HOW TO CROCHET

Learn the Basic Stitches
and Techniques

Sara Delaney

Storey Publishing

*The mission of Storey Publishing is to serve our customers by
publishing practical information that encourages
personal independence in harmony with the environment.*

Edited by Gwen Steege and Kathy Brock
Series design by Alethea Morrison
Art direction by Cynthia N. McFarland and Jeff Stiefel
Text production by Theresa Wiscovitch
Indexed by Eileen Clawson

Cover illustration by © Caitlin Keegan
Interior illustrations by Gayle Isabelle Ford

Storey Publishing
210 MASS MoCA Way
North Adams, MA 01247
www.storey.com

Printed in the United States by McNaughton & Gunn, Inc.
10 9 8 7 6 5 4 3 2 1

LIBRARY OF CONGRESS CATALOGING-IN-PUBLICATION DATA

Delaney, Sara.
  How to crochet / by Sara Delaney.
    pages cm. — (Storey basics)
  Includes index.
  ISBN 978-1-61212-392-9 (pbk. : alk. paper)
  ISBN 978-1-61212-393-6 (e-book) 1. Crocheting. 2. Crocheting—Patterns. I. Title.
TT820.D3957 2014
746.43'4—dc23
                          2014018168

CONTENTS

For Livia Gladu, without you there would be no pages to this book.
Thank you for my first hook, the miles of chains,
and everything else.

GETTING STARTED IN CROCHET

My Memaire taught me to crochet when I was a child because I bugged her. I don't know that I was all that interested in making things at the time; I just wanted to do what she was doing.

And how hard could it be really? She waggled that little hook up and down, wrapped some yarn around it, and poked it into some loops of yarn she'd already made. Surprisingly, I found that it really was, almost, as easy as I thought. There is hook waggling and lots of loops, but in the end the majority of crochet is wrapping yarn around your hook, pulling your hook through loops, and making a choice. You choose with crochet. What stitch do I use and, mostly, where do I put that stitch?

This book will teach you how to read your stitches, how to see them and understand what you're seeing so that you can make the best choice about where to place your next stitch. I also hope you'll learn to love crochet as I do.

BE PREPARED

THE FIRST CHOICES YOU MAKE when you begin any crochet project involve getting prepared, so it's important to assemble all the tools and materials you will need. The success of your project hinges on understanding the materials you're using, as well as knowing their best uses. To avoid the common frustration points in crochet, you need to understand not just how to make your stitches but how the way you use your tools and materials can influence the stitches, as well as the reason you make the stitches in a particular manner and where you place each stitch.

Setting up for a project can seem dry and boring when you're just really excited about getting started, but taking the time to prepare and familiarize yourself with these beginning steps can make all the difference in fending off midproject frustrations, understanding mysteries of gauge and fabric, and preventing the little roadblocks that discourage many newcomers and cause them to give up.

This book will not only teach you the basics of each crochet stitch and how to read your crochet fabric, but it also contains some basic pattern formulas that you can use to make a wide range of beginner projects.

Before You Begin . . .

Patterns are like recipes, so view each one as you would a recipe. Make sure that you have all the materials (the "ingredients") on hand before starting, and familiarize yourself with all the stitches (the "techniques") needed to successfully complete the project (the "dish").

Like any other skill, crochet is something that you build with practice. If this is the first time you've ever picked up a hook and yarn, you will need to dedicate some time and perseverance to learning this new skill. Each time you sit down with your hook and yarn, you will get better, not all at once, but little by little. Be patient with yourself. No one has a natural talent for crochet: They are either just practicing more than you or have been at it longer. And each person has a distinct learning style. Some can read a passage once, understand its full content, and reproduce it easily, while others need repetition, and still others need a visual guide. I'll try to address as many different kinds of learners as I can in this volume to get you started on the crochet path with minimal resistance.

CHAPTER 1

GETTING TO KNOW YOUR MATERIALS

Every person has a basic set of tools needed to complete their job: Batman has his utility belt and cape, the plumber has a monkey wrench and pipe snake. Crocheters have a set of tools too, and knowing how to choose the right tools will make every project that much easier.

THE ONE ESSENTIAL: A HOOK

THE FIRST AND MOST IMPORTANT TOOL to get familiar with is the hook. While it may seem to be one of the simplest tools there is, it can be quite complex. Hooks are available in lots of different materials, and each has a different feel and interacts differently with different yarns. You'll want to experiment to find which materials you like using.

Common Hook Materials

- **Metal.** Most metal hooks are slick and smooth. In fact, they can be quite slippery, allowing the yarn to move very easily over the surface. This type of hook works well with all kinds of yarn.
- **Wood.** Whether made from maple, bamboo, or laminated layers, wooden hooks have a textured surface that gives them a bit more grip on the yarn. If you're working with a slippery yarn, this kind of hook can help you hold on to the yarn and "slow down" the stitches.
- **Plastic.** These hooks are fairly smooth but can have a bit of grip. Depending on what fibers you are crocheting with, you may or may not need the grip.

Parts of the Hook

Whether you are using a tiny steel hook for fine Irish lace or a superlarge hollow plastic hook for rag rugs, the basic parts of the hook are the same. Understanding the anatomy of your hook will help you to better understand the construction of your stitches and help to avoid some pitfalls of gauge and construction. Each manufacturer offers its own combination of the elements described below, and no two companies are alike; many companies even produce more than one style to appeal to a broader audience. No one hook works for every crocheter, and you may need to experiment with several styles before you find the one that is right for you.

- **Point (also sometimes called tip or head) (A).** This is exactly what it sounds like. It is the leading edge of your hook, and it's what will guide you into your next stitch. There is no standard style for this part of the hook. You will find that some manufacturers make hooks with very sharp points and others with fairly blunt, rounded points, as well as everything in between.

- **Throat (B).** This is the tapered portion forming the actual hook that allows for grabbing and pulling the yarn. There are two distinct styles for this section of the hook:
  - **Inline or cut-throat.** These hooks have a solid and straight cylindrical shape all the way around and a notch that has been cut out of the cylinder.
  - **Non-inline or molded.** These hooks have a tapered throat. The cylinder of the hook gets narrower toward the underside of the hook, and the hook itself may be pushed slightly forward from the main cylinder of the hook.
- **Shaft or neck (C).** This is the space between the throat and the thumb rest, or handle, of the hook. The circumference of the shaft is what determines the hook size and is therefore where your stitches should be made.

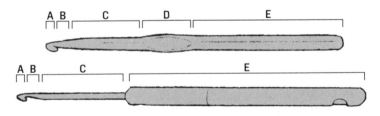

TWO CROCHET HOOK STYLES. Point (A), throat (B), shaft (C), thumb rest (D), handle (E)

- **Thumb rest (D).** This, too, is just what it sounds like: a place for your thumb to rest on the hook. It's an optional element, and some manufacturers do not include it. It's typically where the hook size is noted, even if there is no flattened thumb rest.
- **Handle (E).** The handle may be as simple as a continuation of the hook cylinder or as elaborate as a highly engineered, ergonomic shape meant to fit perfectly into the hand.

Understanding Hook Sizes

Using the correct size hook for your yarn is crucial to a successful project. While you can use very large hooks with very fine yarns to create open, lacy fabric, the opposite is not true. If your hook is too small for your yarn, you will have trouble successfully grabbing the yarn and creating stitches, and you may create a fabric that is too dense for your project. Most modern patterns specify both a hook size and yarn weight to start with. And if you're not working from a pattern, start by using the recommended hook size on your yarn's ball band. (See also

....

Customize Your Hook

Sometimes you just can't find a hook that has all the features you're looking for. Don't be afraid to modify your hooks to better suit you. If you don't like thumb rests, try using the rubber grips made for pencils to change the shape of that part of your hook. If you need a larger handle, use inexpensive polymer clay to build a handle that perfectly suits your own hand!

....

the Craft Yarn Council's Standard Yarn Weight System, which contains suggestions for appropriate hooks for a range of yarn weights, on page 13.)

Hook sizes can be noted in three different ways. Look for the size embossed on the thumb rest or marked elsewhere on the hook. It looks a bit like this: G/6/4.00. The letter and middle number are the American (US) size, and not every hook has a corresponding letter. The number with the decimal is the actual metric measurement of the hook. I recommend checking the metric size of the hook you intend to use against what is recommended in your pattern. US hook sizes aren't necessarily consistent, with the designation G ranging from 4.25 to 4.5 or even 4.75 mm, depending on the manufacturer.

....

A Crocheter's Toolbox

To fill out your crocheter's toolbox you'll want to have the following:

- Tapestry needles for weaving in your tails
- Small sharp scissors
- Small tape measure
- Stitch markers that you can open and close in some way. Split-ring stitch markers, carabiner, or locking ring stitch markers work best. In a pinch you can even use paper clips!
- Small notebook and pen or pencil to make notes

All these things can be kept in a hook case with pockets or in a separate small pouch or container that you keep in your project bag.

....

How to Hold Your Hook

No two crocheters use the hook in the same manner, but there are two main ways to hold the hook while you crochet, and infinite slight variations on each.

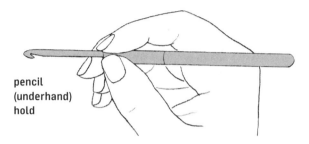

pencil
(underhand)
hold

- **Pencil, or underhand.** Here, the hook is held "above" the hand like you would hold a pencil or paintbrush. When holding the hook like this, most of the moving or manipulation of the hook happens by bending your fingers and rolling the hook between them.
- **Knife, or overhand.** Here the hook is held under the hand as you would hold a knife for cutting. When holding the hook in this manner, most hook manipulation happens with your wrist. Holding the hook like this takes advantage of the thumb rest.

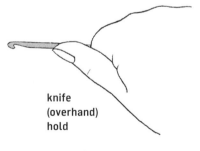

knife
(overhand)
hold

THE YARNS WE LOVE TO USE

THE SECOND MOST IMPORTANT THING you'll need for crochet is yarn. Yarn choices are almost infinite. In today's market, you can find yarns made from nearly every material you can imagine. Traditional wool and cotton have been joined by new fibers synthesized from milk proteins, corn, and soy, as well as animal fibers from bison, chinchillas, and wild possum. You also have a huge range of sizes, or weights, to choose from, starting as small as fine sewing threads and going all the way to superbulky, ropelike yarns. (For guidance, see the Craft Yarn Council's Standard Yarn Weight System, on page 13.)

All that variety can be quite confusing and discouraging when you're just starting out, so keep it simple as you work your way through this book. Since you'll need a lot of practice for most of the stitches you're learning, I recommend choosing a worsted-weight or DK-weight cotton — mercerized perle cotton — if you can find it. Not only is this material and weight easy to work with, you'll also be able to use many of your practice swatches as washcloths. Cotton is also fairly forgiving if

....

Perle Cotton

Mercerized perle (or pearl) cotton has gone through a chemical treatment process that plumps the fibers. As a result, the cotton takes dyes better, for more vibrant and long-lasting colors, and has a shiny or pearled finish.

....

you have to pull stitches out a few times to get them right. My favorite yarns for learning stitches are Cotton Classic by Tahki Stacy Charles yarns and Lily's Sugar 'n Cream. Just be sure to choose a solid color to start; variegated or mixed-color yarns make it harder for you to see your stitches when you're first starting.

Yarn Packaging

Yarn comes packaged in four standard forms:

- **Cones.** Yarn presented on cones means you get lots of yardage and pay slightly less, because winding yarns into smaller packages means higher costs for the manufacturer. Coned yarns are great for larger projects because you won't have lots of ends to work in.
- **Skeins.** This is an elongated version of the ball that can be worked by pulling the yarn from the center or working from the outside.

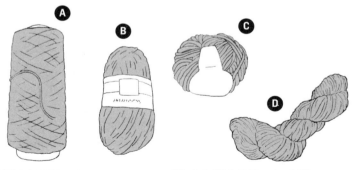

YARN CAN COME PACKAGED as a cone (A), skein (B), ball (C), or hank (D).

- **Balls.** Just as it sounds, this is a ball of yarn that can be worked by pulling the yarn from either the center or the outside.
- **Hanks.** Both handspinners and commercial manufacturers often wind yarn into a large loop or circle (usually about 2 yards in circumference) containing multiple strands, then twist and fold it to make a neat package. You can't crochet directly from the hank; you need to place the circle of yarn over the back of a chair, around the hands of a friend, or on a special winding tool called a swift. Then you can wind the yarn into a ball before you work with it.

A Note on Skeins and Hanks

The word *skein* is often used interchangeably for every presentation of yarn, but it's important to know the differences. If you're ordering yarn online and do not own a swift and ball winder or are not interested in having to wind your yarn by hand before you can begin using it, then you may want to avoid yarn presented in hanks.

Yarn Weights

Yarn also comes in a range of weights; this does not refer to the physical weight of the yarn ball but to the yarn's diameter. You'll find everything from cobweb weight (finer than some sewing threads!) all the way up to superbulky weights that make ropes look thin. The Craft Yarn Council has developed a standard yarn weight system that is a useful starting point, especially when you aren't working from a pattern.

Standard Yarn Weight System

	0 LACE	1 SUPER FINE	2 FINE	3 LIGHT	4 MEDIUM	5 BULKY	6 SUPER BULKY
TYPE OF YARNS IN CATEGORY	FINGERING, 10-COUNT CROCHET THREAD	SOCK, FINGER-ING, BABY	SPORT, BABY	DK, LIGHT WORSTED	WORSTED, AFGHAN, ARAN	CHUNKY, CRAFT, RUG	BULKY, ROVING
CROCHET GAUGE* (number of single crochet stitches to 4")	32–42 double crochets**	21–32	16–20	12–17	11–14	8–11	5–9
RECOMMENDED HOOK in METRIC size range (mm)	Steel*** 1.6–1.4	2.25–3.5	3.5–4.5	4.5–5.5	5.5–6.5	6.5–9	9 and larger
RECOMMENDED HOOK in US size range	Steel*** 6, 7, 8; Regular hook B-1	B-1 to E-4	E-4 to 7	7 to I-9	I-9 to K-10½	K-10½ to M-13	M-13 and larger

*   The above ranges reflect the most commonly used gauges and hook sizes for specific yarn categories.

** Laceweight yarns are usually crocheted on larger hooks to create lacy, openwork patterns. Accordingly, a gauge range is difficult to determine. Always follow the gauge stated in your pattern.

*** Steel crochet hooks are sized differently from regular hooks: the higher the number, the smaller the hook, which is the reverse of regular hook sizing.

Courtesy of the Craft Yarn Council (www.craftyarncouncil.com)

How Do I Hold My Yarn?

Like the way to hold the hook, there's quite a bit of variation in the way crocheters hold their yarn. Typically, you hold your hook and yarn in opposite hands. The hand that holds the yarn controls the tension. ("Tension" describes how loosely or how tautly the yarn is held as it flows into the work.) That's not to say that you should be pulling on it, but you need to have just a bit of tension in the yarn in order to keep your stitches even. Slack yarn — or, conversely, yarn that is pulled tight — results in uneven stitches and makes it difficult to work stitches in subsequent rows. You need just enough tension to allow you to move the yarn forward through your hand to create new stitches, while at the same time feeling some resistance when you pull on that yarn, to make grabbing it with the hook a smooth process.

The drawings that follow show two common ways to tension your yarn.

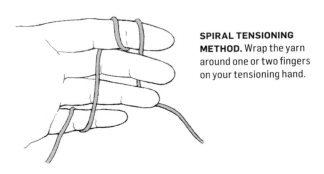

SPIRAL TENSIONING METHOD. Wrap the yarn around one or two fingers on your tensioning hand.

BASKETWEAVE TENSIONING METHOD.
Weave the yarn between the fingers of
your tensioning hand.

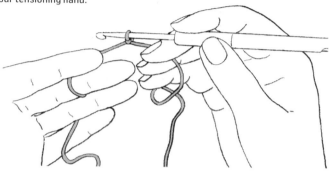

In the end there is no right or wrong combination of the steps and tools in this chapter. Each crocheter is an individual, and your choices and processes should reflect this.

BECOMING A CROCHETER

I HEAR LOTS OF PEOPLE TELL ME that they don't have the patience or the talent for crochet. I don't either! What I do have is an interest in this craft and years of practice under my belt. Spend some time with your yarn and hooks, spend time with other yarns and your hooks. Spend time with someone else's hooks! There's no prerequisite, no underlying gift that makes you a good crocheter. It's an urge to know more, an accumulation of learned skills, and knowledge and time spent in practice.

CHAPTER 2

GETTING STARTED:
FORGET THE CHAIN!

If anyone has tried to teach you to crochet before, they've probably started with chains. Great, those are important — you need them to start almost every crochet project you will make. I feel, however, that making chains is the absolute worst way to begin learning how to crochet, so in this chapter, we're going to skip right to the good stuff.

To obtain a base into which you can crochet, go to the craft or fabric store and buy yourself a ¼ yard or remnant piece of tulle. I know this sounds weird, but trust me, this gives you something to anchor your first row of stitches instead of the usual chain, which is harder to manage. Instead of learning how to make a chain and how to work into it, you can start actual crochet immediately by learning to make single crochet stitches.

EASING INTO SINGLE CROCHET

LOOK FOR A TULLE WITH a very large and open mesh. Bring your crochet hook with you when you shop (H hook for your practice) and see if it will pass through the fabric easily. A perfect fit isn't necessary, and if you tear the tulle a bit as you work, don't worry. This is just for practice!

The yarn for this practice piece should be worsted or dk weight. These middle-of-the-road yarns are the most common weights and will easily pass through a large-mesh tulle.

I describe the way to make a single crochet stitch step-by-step on page 19, but here's an overview of the process: Working from right to left along the upper, long edge of the tulle and starting at the edge in the upper right-hand corner, stick your hook through the fabric. Now take your yarn and fold it in half about 6 to 8 inches from the end, making a loop. Grab that loop with your hook and pull it through the fabric just a bit, not all the way through. You now have one loop on your hook.

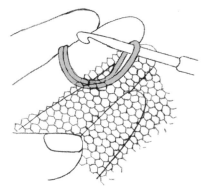

PULL A LOOP through the upper edge of the tulle.

Tilt the work forward a bit so that you can look at the back of it. You'll notice two strands of yarn hanging down. The short one is the *tail*, and the long one (the one connected to your ball or skein) is the *working yarn*. For the next step, don't use the tail; leave it dangling! Instead, grab the working yarn and bring it up over the hook toward yourself (this is a *yarn over*) (A), and slowly and carefully catch that yarn in the throat of the hook and pull it to the right, through the loop that was already on your hook (B). You're now all set and ready to start your first row of single crochet stitches.

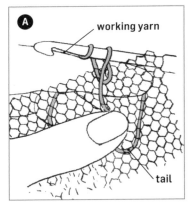
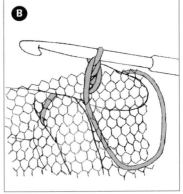

Because crochet is worked from right to left, stick your hook back through the edge of the fabric, about ¼ inch to the left of the last spot you went through. Grab your working yarn with the hook, and pull it through the fabric. You now have two loops on your hook (C). Bring the yarn up and over the hook toward yourself as before (another yarn over), catch the yarn in the throat of the hook, and carefully pull it through both loops that are already on your hook. You just made your first single crochet stitch. Congratulations!

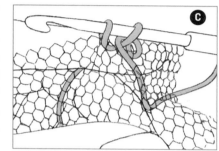

Now do it again — and again. You'll have to do each stitch hundreds or thousands of times to build anything useful, but each time you do, you'll get better at it.

SINGLE CROCHET STEP-BY-STEP

Step 1. Insert your hook through the fabric ¼" to the left of the last spot.

Step 2. Yarn over and pull it through the fabric (2 loops on your hook).

Step 3. Yarn over again.

Step 4. Pull it through both loops on your hook. Stitch done!

There are quite a few different stitches in crochet, but the four most commonly used, and those we discuss in this book, are the single crochet, half double crochet, double crochet, and treble crochet. We'll get into the finer points of all these basic stitches in later chapters, but for now just keep repeating these four steps across until you reach the upper left-hand corner of the fabric, completing your first row of single crochet.

WHY A TURNING CHAIN?

ONCE YOU'VE WORKED YOUR FIRST ROW of stitches, you'll need to add a turning chain before you can begin the next row. (This is true whether you're working into fabric or into a foundation chain, which we'll discuss in a later chapter.) The need for a turning chain is due to a basic characteristic of crochet: Each stitch is built from the bottom up, but your hook has to be waiting at the top before you can begin the next stitch. Otherwise your first stitch will be short and slanted and really hard to find when you come back to it in the next row.

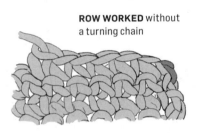

ROW WORKED without a turning chain

Single crochet stitches are almost square, approximately equal in height and width. A single crochet stitch is one stitch wide and one stitch tall. In order to get the hook to the right place to begin the next row of single crochet stitches, your hook needs to be one stitch above where it is now. To accomplish this, you make a turning chain.

MAKING A TURNING CHAIN

Step 1. At the end of the row, yarn over and pull it through the loop that is already on your hook. This is the turning chain.

Step 2. Turn your piece over to start the next row. Since crochet is always worked from right to left, you need to flip the whole piece over like you're turn-ing a page in a book. Your hook should now be at the height of one single chain above the top right-hand corner.

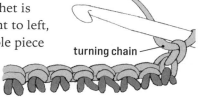

turning chain

Turning Chain Math

Turning chains are necessary to raise your hook to the proper height to begin making the stitches in your next round or row. Depending on the stitch you are beginning the row with, you could start with a chain 1 (for single crochet), 2 (for half double and double crochet), 3 (for double crochet and treble crochet), or 4 (for treble crochet). If you're making up a simple pattern, you can choose how many turning chains to use for double and treble crochet stitches based on the look. If you're working from a pattern, it's best to use what the designer calls for.

CROCHETING INTO EXISTING STITCHES

AT THE BEGINNING OF THE NEXT ROW, instead of working into that easy mesh tulle fabric, you have actual stitches to work into. Let's take a look at what you have in order to determine which stitch to work in first. You'll see what looks like a chain running along the top of that row you just finished: two strands across the top of each stitch that originate and terminate through the two strands from the stitches on either side. There is a front loop — the strand closest to you — and a back loop — the strand farther away. There are also two legs to the stitch. Notice that what you see is actually the back of the stitches that you made in the last row.

READY TO BEGIN row 2, as seen from the top

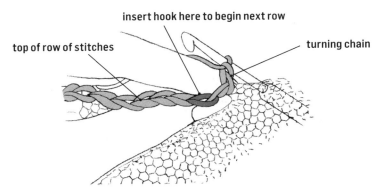

insert hook here to begin next row

top of row of stitches

turning chain

SINGLE CROCHET INTO EXISTING STITCHES

Step 1. Insert your hook under both strands at the top of the first stitch. Make a single crochet stitch following the same steps as when you were working through the tulle fabric: yarn over and bring up a loop, yarn over again, and pull through both loops on your hook. The first single crochet of the second row is made.

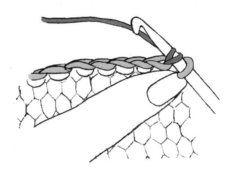

Step 2. Continue to make a single crochet in each of the "chains" (the tops of the stitches) marching their way to the left. Take care to work under both strands at the top of the stitch just as you did in step 1.

Step 3. When you reach the other end, make another turning chain as you did at the end of Row 1, turn the work over, and work your way back. Continue to repeat this row over and over.

PRACTICE MAKES PERFECT

YOU MAY NOTICE THAT YOUR EDGES are funny, and they may be slanting in or out. Don't worry about that for now; we're going to revisit single crochet stitches in chapter 4. For now, just keep practicing this stitch again and again. I recommend spending at least 30 minutes a day practicing your single crochet stitch for a whole week. Feel free to break it up into 10-minute segments, with your coffee in the morning, on your lunch break, in the evening while you watch the news, or any other time you can sit quietly and concentrate on the work.

Each time you sit down to crochet, you'll gain more experience, and it will be easier. It takes about eight hours of performing a new fine-motor skill before your muscle memory kicks in and your brain and muscles remember for you how to perform the stitch. Then you can move on to thinking about the where and why of your stitch placement and construction. Take the time to build this foundation, and the following chapters will present you with much less frustration. Being comfortable making a single crochet stitch and not having to think about it makes everything else in this book seem like a piece of cake!

CHAPTER 3

CHAINS:
YOUR FOUNDATION

Almost every project you will ever make begins with chain stitches. While it's not the sexiest stitch, it is necessary. To get started you'll need to anchor the yarn on your hook; the best way to do this is with a quick *slip knot*.

THE FIRST STEP: MAKING A SLIP KNOT

Step 1. Make a loop with the yarn about 6" from the end. Notice in the drawing that the working yarn is *under* the tail.

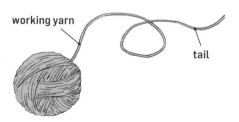

working yarn

tail

Step 2. Slide the tail behind the loop you made in step 1.

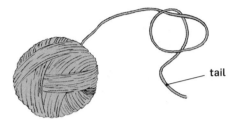

tail

Step 3. Insert the crochet hook under just the tail, and pull the working yarn to tighten.

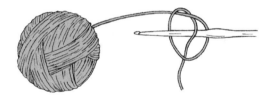

Step 4. Tighten the loop until it is just shy of snug — not so loose that you can see through the loop even as it is on the hook, but not so tight that it can't slide freely on the hook.

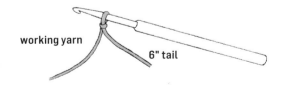

working yarn

6" tail

With the slip knot completed, you will see the two strands of yarn hanging down from the hook. The short one is called the *tail* and should be at least 6 inches long. Move your slip knot farther along if it's coming up shorter than that. You do not use the tail again. The length still connected to your ball or skein is called the *working yarn*. This strand is the yarn that will be worked with your hook to form the crochet fabric. Notice that the slip knot, and all subsequent loops on your hook, have an upside-down teardrop shape.

Managing the Slip Knot

To keep your slip knot from swinging around your hook when you begin to work the chain, you'll need to hold onto it or anchor it in some way to keep it steady. You can try pinching the base of the knot between the thumb and first finger of your left hand. Don't pull; just use gentle, steady pressure.

MAKING THE CHAIN STITCH

Step 1. Holding the hook in your right hand and the yarn in your left, bring the yarn up from behind the hook, over the top, and forward toward yourself (yarn over). You now should have 2 loops on your hook.

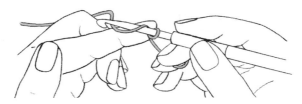

Step 2. Pull the hook to the right, catching the new loop in the throat of the hook, and gently pull it through the old loop, bringing you back to one loop. You've just made your first chain stitch.

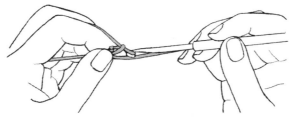

It's important that the hook change position, either by rotating your wrist or rolling the hook between your fingers, for the pull through in this step to happen successfully. The throat of your crochet hook should face you as you make the yarn over in order to "catch" the yarn. Once you catch the yarn, however, you need to rotate the hook 90° clockwise (downward) to ease the passage of the hook through the slip knot or the previous loop. Study the position of the hook in the illustration to see how this works.

Step 3. Repeat steps 1 and 2. With one loop on your hook, yarn over, and pull the new loop through the old one. Each time you complete steps 1 and 2 you should have just one loop remaining on your hook.

EVALUATING YOUR CHAIN

CONTINUE TO MAKE MORE CHAINS, watching your chain grow in length below your hook. Practice this for a while. It may not seem like much, but your eyes, hands, and mind are learning how to coordinate and complete this new skill together. Once you've got a few inches of chain done, stop and look at it for a few minutes. You're likely to notice the following:

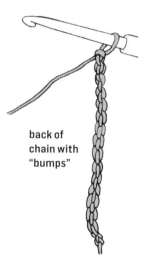

back of chain with "bumps"

- **It is not even and pretty.** Don't be too hard on it. That's totally normal; you're just learning how to do this, and you're probably not very coordinated yet. No worries! It gets better and easier with practice.

- **It has two sides.** If you run the length of the chain between your fingers, you'll feel two distinct sides: There is a flat smooth side; this is the front, and it looks like a length of chain. Then there is a bumpy side; this is the back of the chain.
- **Each chain stitch has three parts.** Any one of these parts — the top loop, the bottom loop, and the back loop — may be referred to in crochet directions, so it's good to get to know them.

....

Size Matters

Make sure that you're slipping each completed chain stitch up onto the neck of the hook, the section of the hook that determines the gauge of your stitches. If you keep the chain loops down in the throat of the hook, which is narrower than the neck, you will have difficulty getting your hook back into these stitches in subsequent rows.

....

COUNTING CHAIN STITCHES

Now is a good time to learn how to count the stitches you've made. It's important to remember that the loop that remains on your hook between stitches *never* counts! This loop is "potential" and will become part of the next stitch you make, but it is never a stitch on its own. The drawing below shows a length of chain in progress, with each chain numbered and the shape of one full chain stitch highlighted. Note that the numbers begin at the hook and work back to the slip knot. When working in small amounts, it's easiest to count back from your hook.

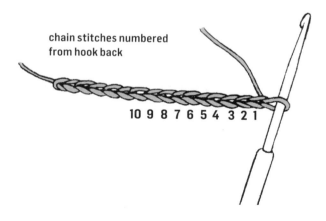

chain stitches numbered
from hook back

10 9 8 7 6 5 4 3 2 1

CHAPTER 4

BASIC CROCHET STITCHES

Each of the four most common stitches has a wonderful purpose and beauty all its own. With a few flicks of your wrist and fingers you can create a dense and heavy fabric or a light open mesh.

Single crochet gives you a solid fabric with great structure and a smooth surface that is a great background for embellishments and embroidery. Half doubles give you a finished fabric with more movement but still present a solid surface while accumulating faster than singles. Double crochet stitches have a wonderful rhythm all their own and quickly become the favorite stitch of many crocheters, both for the speed with which the stitches build into fabric and the easy airy fabric that these stitches can create. Trebles are long and leggy and can create a wonderful mesh fabric in little time. You'll find your favorite uses for each stitch with time and practice.

BEGINNING TO WORK FROM A FOUNDATION CHAIN

IN THIS CHAPTER YOU'LL PULL TOGETHER the last two skills you've learned: chains and single crochet. Now that you understand how to make a chain and its basic anatomy, you can use it as a foundation in which to place your stitches, instead of into the tulle that we used earlier. We'll start with our friend the single crochet stitch. You know how to make this stitch in established stitches (see page 23), but in this section you'll learn how to anchor it in a foundation chain and also discover how to recognize it in your fabric.

Deconstructing the First Stitch into a Foundation Chain

Let's work on a piece that isn't too wide so you can hit the tricky bits more often and practice the process. A practice swatch that is 10 single crochet stitches wide is perfect, so go ahead and make a foundation chain that is 11 chains long.

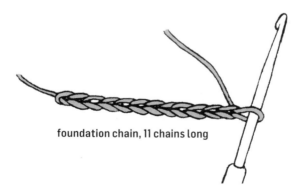

foundation chain, 11 chains long

Wait a minute! Didn't I just say that we were going to work a swatch that was 10 single crochet stitches wide? I did! But the rule with *foundation chains* (as opposed to working into existing stitches) is that you need to add the turning chain (see page 20) to the foundation chain before you begin the first row of stitches. So, if we want a swatch that is 10 single crochet stitches wide, and the turning chain for single crochet is one chain, then our foundation chain has to be 11 chains long: $10 + 1 = 11$.

To locate the place to put your hook for the first stitch into the foundation chain, count back from your hook (remember that the loop on the hook *does not* count) to the second chain from the hook. This is the chain where you will make your first single crochet stitch, following the instructions on page 23.

Why did we go to the second chain from the hook and not just the first one? There are two reasons:

- The loop on your hook, the one that isn't an actual stitch yet, is what holds the previous stitch together. If you go back into the first chain from the hook you'll just be remaking the same loop that already exists. And you'll end up with one long, loose loop on your hook.
- When you skip the first chain from the hook, it becomes your turning chain. Your hook is now one stitch above the foundation chain, perfectly placed to begin a row of single crochet stitches.

Working into Foundation Chain Stitches

There are three different ways you can work into a chain stitch. We'll start with the easiest first.

- **Under the top strand.** Insert your hook just under the top strand of the chain to anchor your stitch. This is the easiest method. Using only one strand of the chain leaves the other two strands of yarn free along the edge, which makes a more flexible chain edge.

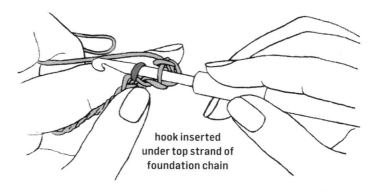

hook inserted
under top strand of
foundation chain

- **Under the back bump.** Insert your hook under the bump that makes up the back of the chain stitch. This method also leaves the chain edge more flexible as two strands of each chain are left unworked, but it can be harder to read the stitches and find the correct strand to work under. On the plus side, this method gives you an edge that most effectively resembles the finished top edge of a row of stitches. If you are looking for two edges with the same appearance at the beginning and end of your project, this is the method to use.

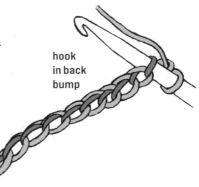

hook in back bump

hook in top and bottom strands

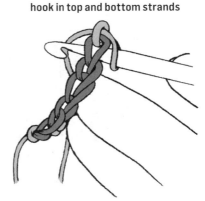

• **Under both the top and bottom strands.** Insert your hook under both strands that make up the front of the chain. This is the most difficult of the three. It can be quite tricky to get your hook under both strands of the front of the chain, and it makes for a very firm and inflexible chain edge. On the plus side, it leaves you with almost no evidence that there ever was a foundation chain.

Each of these methods has its uses, but for the purposes of this book, I'll always be referring to the first method (under the top strand) when I talk about working into a foundation chain.

WORKING SINGLE CROCHET IN A FOUNDATION CHAIN

Step 1. Insert your hook under the top strand of the second chain from the hook. Yarn over and pull up a loop, yarn over again, and pull through the 2 remaining loops on your hook. (See page 22 if you need a refresher.)

Step 2. Continue in this manner, inserting your hook under the top strand of the next chain and then completing a single crochet stitch. Work your way across until you have completed 10 single crochets.

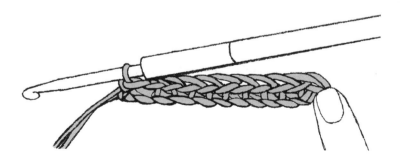

Analyzing Your First Row

Take a minute to look at the stitches you've made in your foundation chain. You'll see that each stitch has two legs that come down, and their "toes" are almost pointed together before they disappear through the foundation chain and form a V shape. You'll also see that each stitch has what looks like a new chain across the top of it; this is the *right ("front") side* of the stitch itself.

Now, make one turning chain and turn the work over. Look at each stitch again on the other side. Notice that the two legs point away from each other and there is an extra strand horizontally across the legs under the chain at the top. This is the *wrong side* of the stitch. It looks a bit like the pi symbol (π).

π **1 stitch**

SINGLE CROCHET, with one wrong-side stitch highlighted

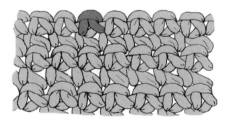

Work a few rows, turning and working in the same way you did when practicing with tulle in chapter 2, and then take a look at the piece you've been building. Notice that, as described earlier, the right and wrong sides of your stitches are shaped differently. You'll see alternating rows of those shapes in your piece. At a quick glance, it's easy to mistake these two rows as a single row of work, like stacked Lincoln Logs, but if you look closer you will see the right- and wrong-side row pattern.

Keeping Track

To help you identify where the last stitch should go, and to avoid inadvertently increasing or decreasing stitches at the edges, always put a stitch marker in the first stitch of each row so that you know when you've reached the last stitch. When you're a new crocheter, it's also important to count your stitches at the end of each row to confirm that the number remains the same from row to row. You can also count as you work.

STITCH MARKER inserted in first stitch

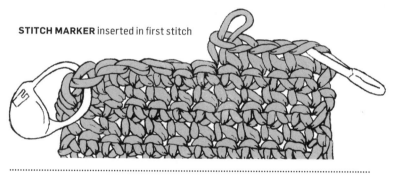

A Few Thoughts about Crochet Anatomy

Alternating rows. When you crochet, you are always creating the stitches with the right side facing you. There is no way to create a crochet stitch in reverse, so you cannot alternate right- and wrong-side stitches in the same row. When you turn the piece over to work the next row, you are working the right side of your new stitches into the wrong side of the row below. You always have alternating rows of right- and wrong-side stitches with crochet no matter what stitch you are using. The only exception to this rule is when you work in the round, which we'll discuss in chapter 6.

Non-aligned columns. Another important thing to understand about crochet stitches in general is that they don't line up in nice columns. The stitches in each row are offset by a half stitch; they stack up like bricks on a wall. This is the case because when you insert your hook under the two strands at the top of the stitch, you are actually placing your hook between two stitches. This results in a slightly scalloped effect on your left and right edges, which is perfectly normal and can be straightened with edge stitches and blocking, which are also discussed in later chapters.

HALF DOUBLE CROCHET

BEFORE YOU BEGIN LEARNING any of the additional stitches in this book, it's important to understand that you've already done most of the hard work! This and the following stitches are not entirely new; they build on the knowledge you already have.

The best and easiest way to practice any new stitch is not to start with a foundation chain but to work your new stitches into existing stitches, so we'll start by working a swatch.

WORKING HALF DOUBLE CROCHET

Setup step 1. Start with a foundation chain of 11. Work 2 rows of single crochet (10 stitches in each row).

Setup step 2. Half double crochet stitches are one-and-a-half times as tall as a single crochet stitch, so you need 2 turning chains before beginning each row of half double crochet stitches. Chain 2 and turn to begin a new row.

Step 1. There is an extra step to the half double crochet stitch: You need to yarn over *before* you begin the stitch.

So, yarn over and insert your hook into the first stitch (the same first stitch you would have chosen with single crochet).

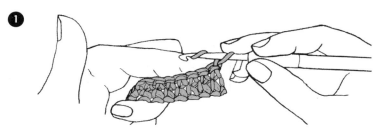

Step 2. Yarn over again, and bring up a loop. You now have 3 loops on your hook.

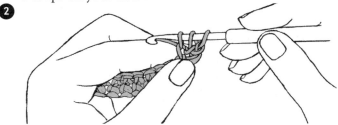

Step 3. Yarn over again and pull through all 3 loops: half double crochet complete!

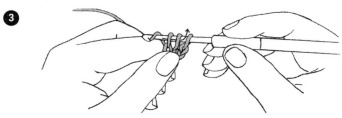

Finish this first row by repeating steps 1 through 3 in each stitch across, then chain 2, and turn the work over. You'll notice that these stitches look different from what you're used to seeing with single crochet. At first glance, it looks like the two strands at the top of the stitch, the ones that look like a chain, are facing you (see top illustration below). Don't be fooled! The bottom strand of that chain facing you is actually from the new yarn over that you worked at the beginning of the stitch, and the top strand is the front loop at the top of the stitch. If you rotate the piece toward yourself, you'll see that the two strands at the top of the stitch are still at the top, angled slightly away from you. You'll continue to work under those top two strands. Just practice this stitch for a few rows to get the rhythm of it.

WRONG-SIDE ROW
highlighted

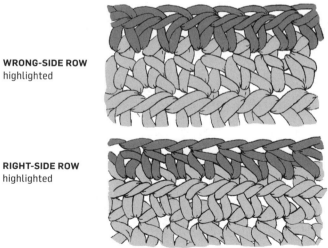

RIGHT-SIDE ROW
highlighted

Analyzing Half Double Crochet

Now that you've got a few rows of half double crochet stitches done, let's take a look at them. Keep in mind that, just as with single crochet stitches, you're looking at alternating rows of the right and wrong sides of the stitches. With your hook at the top left-hand corner (so you know you're looking at the right side of these stitches), look at the row you've just completed. You can see the two strands at the top of the stitch that look like a chain, and under those, three strands seem to chase each other around in a triangle.

You'll also notice that if you slip your hook under the top two strands of the stitch, there is a third strand between the vertical portion of the stitches that is now under your hook. Now look two rows below that to see another right-side row that has a row of stitches worked into it. The chain from the top is missing, but you can still see the triangle.

HALF DOUBLE CROCHET, with right-side rows highlighted

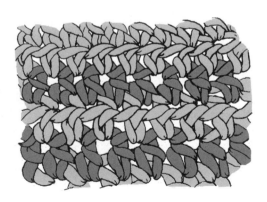

Now, flip the piece over, keeping your hook in the upper right-hand corner, and take a look at the wrong side of your stitches. There's that fake "chain" that makes up the upper half of the stitch, and then you can see two strands that form a V, very similar to how the right side of a single crochet stitch looks. Look two rows below that to see another wrong-side row that has a row of stitches worked into it. The chain has been reduced to just the bottom strand, giving you a bit of a wavy ridge along the top of that row with the V still intact below it.

HALF DOUBLE CROCHET, with wrong-side rows highlighted

Top Tip

When a crochet stitch is completed, the top of the stitch (the two chainlike strands that you anchor the next row to) are actually just to the right of the *post* (the vertical section) of the stitch. This is true for every stitch. It's hard to see in the single crochet stitch, as it almost becomes part of the previous stitch, but it's easier to see as your stitches get taller, that is, with the double and treble crochet stitches covered later in this chapter.

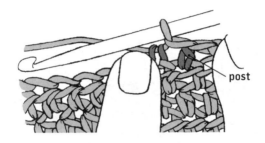

post

WORKING HALF DOUBLE CROCHET INTO A FOUNDATION CHAIN

Setup step 1. Start with a piece that isn't too wide: a practice swatch that is 10 half double crochet stitches wide is perfect.

Setup step 2. Make your foundation chain 12 chains long. (For a swatch that is 10 half double crochet stitches wide, you need 2 turning chains, so our foundation chain has to be 12 chains long: 10 + 2 = 12.)

Step 1. On the foundation chain, count back from your hook (remember that the loop on the hook does not count) to the 3rd chain from your hook. This is the chain where you will make your first half double crochet stitch; the 2 chains you skipped are the turning chain for this first row.

Steps 2–4. Follow steps 1–3 on pages 41–42 to make the half double crochet stitch along the foundation chain, inserting your hook under the top strand of the next chain to begin each stitch. Work your way across until you have completed 10 half double crochets. You may want to practice the foundation chain and this row a few times.

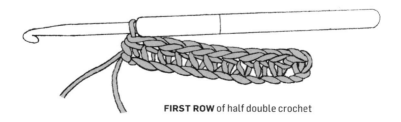

FIRST ROW of half double crochet

DOUBLE CROCHET

DOUBLE CROCHET STITCHES are an additional half stitch taller than half double crochet stitches, and they are actually twice the height of single crochet stitches. You therefore still need 2 turning chains before beginning each row of stitches. Also, not only do you yarn over before you begin the stitch, but there is an extra yarn over to finish it. Once again, start by practicing your new stitch into existing stitches.

WORKING DOUBLE CROCHET

Setup step 1. Begin a practice swatch: work an 11-stitch foundation chain, then work 2 rows of single crochet into it (10 stitches in each row).

Setup step 2. Chain 2 (turning chains) and turn your work over to begin the new row.

Step 1. Yarn over and insert your hook into the first stitch (the same stitch you would use for single crochet).

Step 2. Yarn over again, and bring up a loop. You now have 3 loops on your hook.

Step 3. Yarn over again and pull through only 2 of the loops; this leaves you with 2 loops on your hook.

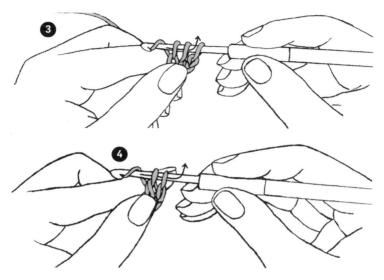

Step 4. Yarn over again and pull through the remaining 2 loops: double crochet complete.

Step 5. Finish this first row of double crochet, chain 2, and turn the work over.

When you turn the piece over, you'll notice that these double crochet stitches look different from what you've gotten used to with single or half double crochet. Again, you'll see what looks like a chain in the top half of the stitch, but this time with an extra strand looping underneath and between each "chain." The bottom half of the stitch looks like two opposite-facing parentheses locked into each other, and there's the same V that we saw with the half double crochet

WORKING DOUBLE CROCHET, continued

stitch. There are nice open spaces between these stitches, and it would be so easy to slip your hook through there and call it a day, but don't be lured in by the Siren song of the space. You still work under only the top two strands. Practice this stitch for a few more rows to get the rhythm of it.

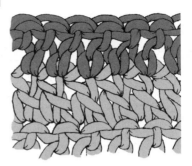

DOUBLE CROCHET, with wrong-side row highlighted

Analyzing Double Crochet

Now that you've got a few rows of double crochet stitches done, let's take a look at them. Keep in mind that just as with previous stitches, you'll be looking at alternating rows of the right and wrong sides of the stitches.

- With your hook at the top left-hand corner (so you know you're looking at the right side of these stitches), look at the row you've just completed. You can see the two strands at the top of the stitch that look like a chain, and under those you'll see two strands that form a V. This V terminates in the same three strands that seem to chase each other around in a triangle that we saw in the half double crochet stitch (A).

- Look two rows below that to see another right-side row that has a row of stitches worked into it. The chain from the top is missing, but you can still see the two strands that form a V terminating in the same three strands that form a triangle (B).

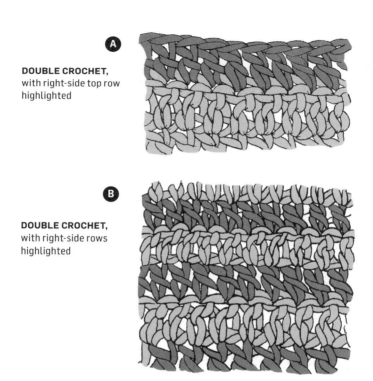

DOUBLE CROCHET, with right-side top row highlighted **A**

DOUBLE CROCHET, with right-side rows highlighted **B**

- Now flip the piece over, with the hook in the upper right-hand corner, and take a look at the wrong side of your stitches. Again you'll see what looks like a chain in the top half and the extra strand looping underneath and between each "chain." The bottom half of the stitch has the opposite facing parenthesis and then the same V that we saw with the half double crochet stitch.

- Look two rows below that to see another wrong-side row that has a row of stitches worked into it. The "chain" has been reduced to just the bottom strand and the third strand that was between the chains, giving you a double dashed line with the parentheses and V still intact below.

WORKING DOUBLE CROCHET INTO A FOUNDATION CHAIN

Setup. A practice swatch 10 double crochet stitches wide is perfect, so begin by making a foundation chain 12 chains long. (Remember that for a swatch that is 10 double crochet stitches wide, you need a turning chain of 2 chains, so your foundation chain has to be 12 chains long.)

Step 1. Count back from your hook to the 3rd chain from your hook. (Remember *not* to count the loop on the hook.) This is where you will make your first double crochet stitch; the 2 chains you skipped become the turning chain for this first row.

Steps 2–5. Follow steps 1–4 on pages 48–50 to work a double crochet stitch.

Continue in this manner, inserting your hook under the top strand of the next chain and then completing a double crochet stitch. Work your way across until you have completed 10 double crochets. Practice the foundation chain and this first row a few times.

TREBLE CROCHET

TREBLE CROCHET STITCHES, also sometimes called triple crochet stitches, are a full two chains taller than single crochet stitches, so we'll need 3 turning chains before we begin each row of stitches. There are also two extra steps to the treble stitch: You yarn over *twice* before you begin the stitch, and there is an extra yarn over to finish it. As usual, let's practice by working this new stitch into existing stitches.

WORKING TREBLE CROCHET

Setup step 1. For your practice swatch, make a foundation chain of 11, and then work 2 rows of single crochet into it (10 stitches in each row).

Setup step 2. Chain 3 and turn your work to begin the new row.

....

Getting the Turning Chain Right

Some patterns will have you work 3 chains for a turning chain with double crochet, and even 4 chains with treble crochet. Be sure to refer to the pattern you are working with and use the number of turning chains indicated by the designer or pattern author.

....

Step 1. Yarn over twice and insert your hook into the first stitch (the same first stitch you would have chosen with all previous stitches).

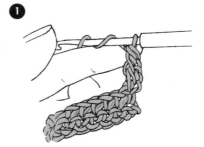

Step 2. Yarn over again, and bring up a loop. You now have 4 loops on your hook.

Step 3. Yarn over again and pull through only 2 of the loops on your hook; this leaves 3 loops on your hook.

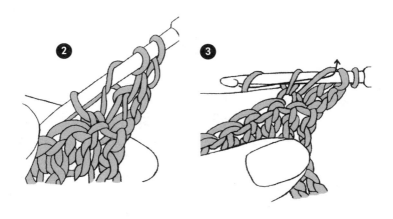

Step 4. Repeat step 3: Yarn over and pull through only 2 of the loops on your hook; this leaves 2 loops on your hook.

Step 5. Yarn over once more and pull through the remaining 2 loops: treble crochet complete. Finish out this first row, chain 3, and turn the work over.

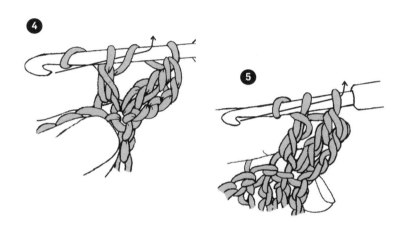

Watch the Space

Treble crochet stitches are very tall and leggy, and it is easy to be fooled into using the space between the stitches to anchor your new row of stitches, but don't! Just work under those top two strands of the stitch. Practice the treble stitch for a few rows to get the rhythm of it.

Analyzing Treble Crochet

Now that you've done a few rows of treble crochet stitches, let's take a look at them. Keep in mind that, just as with previous stitches, you'll see alternating rows of the right side and the wrong side of the stitches.

- Look at the row you've just completed, with your hook at the top left-hand corner so you know you're looking at the right side of this row. You can see the two strands at the top of the stitch that look like a chain, and under those you'll see two strands that form a V that terminates in the same three strands that seem to chase each other around in a triangle (A). This is what we saw in the double crochet stitch (pages 50–51) with that same three-strand triangle.

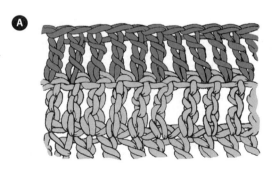

TREBLE CROCHET, with right-side top row highlighted

- Look two rows below that to see another right-side row that has a row of stitches worked into it. The chain from the top is missing but the rest of the stitch is the same: the V and two stacked triangles (B).

B

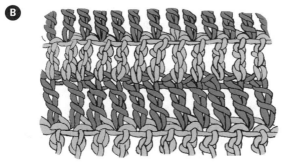

TREBLE CROCHET, with right-side rows highlighted

- Now flip the piece over, hook in the upper right-hand corner, and take a look at the wrong side of your stitches. Again you'll see what looks like a chain in the top half and the extra strand looping underneath and between each "chain." The bottom half of the stitch has two pairs of parentheses and then the V (C).

C

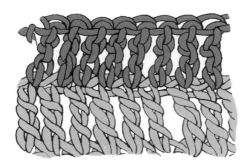

TREBLE CROCHET, with wrong-side top row highlighted

- Look two rows below that to see another wrong-side row that has a row of stitches worked into it. The "chain" has been reduced to just the bottom strand, and that third strand that was between the chains gives you a double dashed line with the pairs of parentheses and the V is still intact below (D).

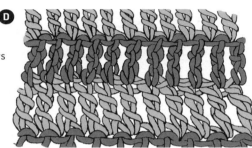

TREBLE CROCHET, with wrong-side rows highlighted

Banish Aches and Pains

Sometimes when you're practicing a new skill, you'll suffer some aches and pains as your body adjusts to the new way in which it is being used. Lots of time spent crocheting or time spent with plant-based fiber, which has little give, can lead to some hand or finger cramping. Try taking a break every 15 minutes or so to gently stretch your hands. If you find your hand cramping around the hook, try using a rubber pencil grip to increase the circumference of the handle and make the hook easier to hold.

WORKING TREBLE CROCHET INTO A FOUNDATION CHAIN

Setup. Start with a practice swatch that is 10 treble crochet stitches wide. The turning chain is 3 chains, so your foundation chain has to be 13 chains long: 10 + 3 = 13.

Step 1. On the foundation chain, count back from your hook to the 4th chain from the hook. (Remember that the loop on the hook does not count.) This is the chain where you will make your first treble

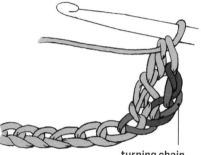

turning chain

crochet stitch; the 3 chains you skipped are the turning chain for this first row.

Steps 2–6. Repeat steps 1–5 on pages 54–55 to work the treble crochet.

Continue in this manner, inserting your hook under the top strand of the next chain and then working a treble crochet stitch. Work your way across until you have completed 10 treble crochets. Practice the foundation chain and just this row a few times. (See illustration on next page.)

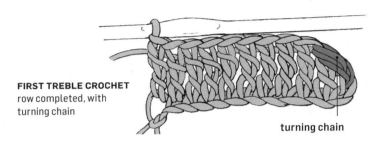

FIRST TREBLE CROCHET
row completed, with
turning chain

turning chain

....

When You Get to the End: Fastening Off

When you've finished a piece, you will want to make sure that it is
securely finished in a way that will not easily unravel. One of the
most wonderful things about crochet is the fact that it *cannot* unravel
from the bottom up! You can cut a hole in the middle of your work
and you will be sad because there's now a hole in your work, but it
won't get any bigger. You would have to unravel it stitch by stitch,
like untying a knot. Every time you place a stitch into your work you
lock the previous stitch and the stitch below it into place. All you
really have to worry about is that the last stitch you make stays in
place, and that's very simple. Once you have finished the last stitch,
you can cut your yarn, leaving at least 6 inches for weaving in. Then
yarn over your hook once more and pull the stitch through the loop
on your hook. Keep pulling until the tail pops out. Give the tail a little
tug, and your work is secure!

....

CHAPTER 5

GAUGE

In the preceding chapters, you've been encouraged to analyze each kind of stitch in order to recognize it and understand its structure. I like to think of this as learning to "read" your stitches, and one of the best ways to reinforce this is to practice measuring the gauge of your piece.

Gauge describes how many stitches and how many rows you are creating per inch with your yarn and hook. While gauge may not be critical for practice swatches or basic pattern formulas where finished size isn't important, it is essential when making any garment or accessory that must fit properly. To ignore the gauge given in the pattern directions may result in your making a sweater that would fit an ogre or a hat that is too small for a newborn.

SWATCHING FOR GAUGE: GETTING STARTED

IT'S BEST TO BEGIN WITH THE YARN and hook recommended in your pattern. If the yarn is no longer available, try to find one with a similar weight and fiber content as the original yarn. Remember that the pattern is only a starting point. Your tension may differ from that of the designer's, and you may therefore need to change your hook size to achieve the correct gauge.

Many patterns tell you to make a 4" × 4" swatch to measure gauge. If you knew how many stitches to chain to get 4 inches, why would you need to swatch?! Start a chain and when it measures just longer than 4 inches you can start working your first row of stitches.

The 4" × 4" measurement is an approximation meant to encourage you to swatch bigger, not smaller. The larger the swatch, the more accurate a measurement of your gauge you will get. To measure your average gauge on your swatch, you should measure over at least 3 inches in several different spots on the swatch. This helps to account for little changes and inconsistencies in your tension. Additionally, if you measure over only 1 inch, you may be inclined to disregard extra fractions of a stitch. For instance, ⅓ of a stitch means a whole extra stitch when measured over 3 inches, and, more startling, over a 30-inch chest measurement, you'd have missed 10 whole stitches! Also, don't measure too close to the edges, where the stitches are likely to be less even.

MEASURING GAUGE

Step 1. Crochet a swatch that measures 4" × 4". You don't need the swatch to be exactly this size, but the larger, the better.

Step 2. Count the number of stitches over 3" and divide by 3. This gives you the number of stitches per inch.

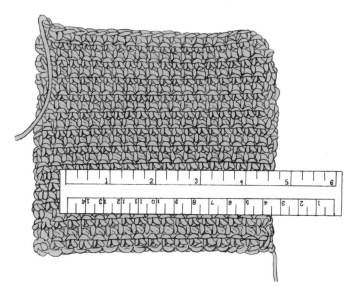

Step 3. Now lay the ruler over the swatch vertically and count the number of rows over 3"; again divide by 3 to get the number of rows per inch.

Step 4. Soak, wash, and block your swatch in the same way
you will be finishing your actual item, then again measure
the stitches and rows per inch. This is an essential step,
because the prewashed swatch does not provide your finished gauge. Compare the two measurements to see how
much, or how little, the yarn changes after blocking. (See
Blocking, page 97, for information.)

WHY DOES GAUGE MATTER?

YOUR NUMBER OF STITCHES PER INCH absolutely must match
the gauge given in the pattern! For example, say you're making
a hat in single crochet that needs to measure 20 inches around.
The pattern specifies a gauge of 5 stitches per inch and tells you
to chain 101, for 100 single crochet stitches. In other words, 5
stitches per inch × 20 inches = 100 stitches total. But what if
your swatch tells you you're crocheting at a different gauge?
Here's what happens if you have fewer or more stitches per inch
than the pattern calls for:

Too few stitches per inch. Your stitch gauge is 4½ stitches per
inch, but you figure it's close enough and keep going.

100 single crochet stitches ÷ 4½ stitches per inch =

22 inches

Your hat is too big!

Too many stitches per inch. Your stitch gauge is 5½ stitches per inch, but you figure it's close enough and keep going, and here's what happens:

$$100 \text{ single crochet stitches} \div 5\frac{1}{2} \text{ stitches per inch} =$$
$$18 \text{ inches}$$

Now your hat is too small!

As you can see, even a half stitch per inch difference in gauge really changes things. On the other hand, row gauge does not have to be spot on, and it frequently just can't be matched, so don't stress about it too much. Most patterns include a schematic (a simple line drawing of the finished item with measurements of each section), or the pattern directs you to work for a certain number of inches. You can easily add or subtract a few rows of stitches to get the correct lengthwise measurements.

Tips for Getting Accurate Gauge

- When you measure, lay your swatch on a flat, hard surface, such as a tabletop. Nonflat surfaces (such as your lap) can give you a false reading.
- Don't pull or push your swatch to get it close to the gauge you want. This, too, will give you a false reading and result in your finished item having the wrong measurements.
- Measure only along the center stitches and rows of your swatch, as edge stitches can be distorted.

MAKING GOOD USE OF YOUR SWATCH

WHEN YOU'RE MEASURING YOUR SWATCH, don't cheat — that never works. When you take the time to swatch properly, not only will you end up with finished items that fit, but you'll also learn how the yarn feels in your hands, how it looks in the stitch pattern, and whether or not you even like it. You may not like the yarn after you've swatched with it, or you may not like working the stitch pattern. Much better to discover this in a little swatch than in the middle of a sweater!

Don't hesitate to reswatch, next time trying a different hook size. Let's revisit that hat project described earlier to see what you can do to arrive at the correct gauge. The hat is worked in single crochet and needs to measure 20 inches around. The pattern specifies 5 stitches per inch and tells you to chain 101 (for 100 single crochet stitches).

If your gauge comes out with too few stitches per inch. For your original swatch, you used the size G/6 (4.00 mm) crochet hook specified by the pattern, but you got too few stitches per inch. In other words, this size hook resulted in stitches that were too big. Try swatching with a smaller hook, such as an F/5 (3.75 mm) crochet hook. On a smaller hook, your stitches will be smaller so that you may get the 5 stitches per inch that you're aiming for.

If your gauge comes out with too many stitches per inch. Your original swatch, crocheted with the G/6 (4.00 mm) hook, had 5½ stitches per inch, too many per inch and too small for the pattern. In this case, the hook was too small, so try reswatching with a larger hook, such as a US size 7 (4.5 mm). On a larger hook, your stitches will be larger and fewer of them will fit into an inch, ideally giving you the 5 stitches per inch you need.

CHECK AND DOUBLE-CHECK

CONTINUE TO CHECK YOUR GAUGE from time to time as you work on your project. Stresses in your life can affect how you make your stitches, including making them larger or smaller, which influences your gauge. Keep your swatches and use them for comparison as you work. If you find that your stitches are getting bigger (too few per inch), you will use more yarn and may even run out before you finish crocheting. Swatches are also great records of projects you've completed, especially if you gift most of your work!

On Hold

When you need to set your work down or pack it away for travel, it's a good idea to secure the live loop on your hook. Slip your hook free from the work and place a locking stitch marker in the

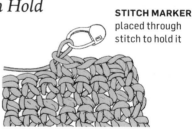

STITCH MARKER
placed through
stitch to hold it

loop. This way the loop can get bigger but cannot be pulled back through the previous loop and unravel the work you've done.

CHAPTER 6

WORKING IN THE ROUND

In chapter 4, you learned how to use a chain as a flat foundation to build your piece upon when you're going to be working back and forth in rows. In this chapter, we take a look at another way of using a chain to begin a project: joining the chain into a ring. This is the approach to take for a project that needs to be worked in the round and requires a central foundation point. Known as a *foundation ring*, this begins with a very short chain, usually between 4 and 12 chain stitches long, with its ends joined to form a ring. Working in the round quite literally means what it says. You work the first round into the center of the ring, *not* into the chain stitches that form the ring.

Whether you are working joined rounds (see page 73) or spiral rounds (see page 80), you start at a central point and work outward. Think of your ring as a doughnut, with the doughnut hole the place where you anchor your stitches. When you work in the round, you are always working with the right side of the stitches facing you.

For practice, let's start with a chain of 10. You're going to turn this short foundation chain into a ring by joining one end to the other with a *slip stitch*. A slip stitch is constructed in much the same way as a chain stitch, but it is used to anchor two stitches together.

CREATING A FOUNDATION RING

Step 1. Bring the chain around into circle shape. (You can see in the drawing that the bottom loop of each chain travels around the outside of this circle.) Insert your hook under the bottom loop of the very first chain.

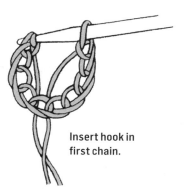

Insert hook in first chain.

Step 2. Yarn over and pull the yarn through both loops on your hook (the first chain and the original loop on your hook). The slip stitch is complete, and the ring is formed. Note the stitch marker. When first beginning to work crochet projects in the

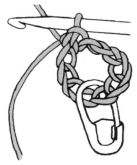

slipstitch to join ring

round, it's a good idea to mark your foundation ring with a stitch marker. When you later begin making the first round of stitches in this ring, it can be hard to distinguish between your foundation ring and the space between your first stitches.

GET THE STITCH HEIGHT AND COUNT RIGHT

Stitch height. The taller the stitch you're working with, the more stitches you need to make in the center of the ring to ensure that your piece stays flat. Single crochet stitches are short, so the circumference of the circle they make won't be very large, and you won't need many of them to fill that space; usually 8 is all you need. Double crochet stitches are twice as tall as single crochet stitches, so they create a circle with nearly double the circumference as one made with single crochet. You'll need to almost double the number of stitches to fill that space, usually 12 to 14.

8 single crochet in ring

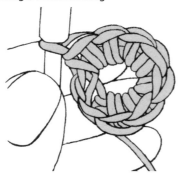

12 double crochet in ring

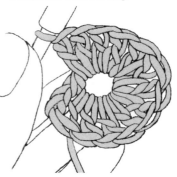

Fitting stitches into the starting ring. There is more room in that little ring than you think, and it's big enough for all your Round 1 stitches. You can really cram the feet of your stitches into that space, and the tops of your stitches will still have plenty of space to spread out and lie flat along the outer edge of the circle you are forming. You can always give yourself a little more room to work into the ring by gently holding the base of the last stitch you made and pulling the ring, like a drawstring.

12 double crochet in ring

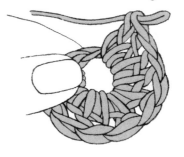

Increases Needed to Maintain a Flat Piece

ROUND	NUMBER OF STITCHES			
	SC	HDC	DC	TR
1	8	10	12	16
2	16	20	24	32
3	24	30	36	48
4	32	40	48	64

Note that you must add the number of stitches that you began with in Round 1 to each additional round, and the number of stitches in Round 1 is determined by the stitch used. For instance, in single crochet, you begin with 8 stitches in the round, so you add 8 stitches in each subsequent round: In Round 2, add 8 to the original 8 to get 16; in Round 3, add 8 to the 16 in Round 2 to get 24; in Round 4 add 8 to the 24 in Round 3 to get 32. The table shows the results for 4 rounds; you can use the following formula to successfully crochet flat circles working any stitch (x = the number of stitches in Round 1):

Rnd 1: x
Rnd 2: x+x = a
Rnd 3: a+x = b
Rnd 4: b+x = c
Rnd 5: c+x = d

Making increases in subsequent rounds. Whatever number of stitches you begin with in Round 1 is exactly how many stitches you must add in each additional round to keep your piece flat. For example, if your pattern begins with 8 stitches in the ring, then you must add 8 additional stitches to every round after that to maintain a flat piece. The table above shows how this works. It's important to note that in Round 3 you do not double your stitches as you do in Round 2. You add only the number of stitches contained in Round 1. This is true no matter how many stitches you begin with, so be sure to take note of the number of stitches you made in that first round.

JOINED ROUNDS

THERE ARE TWO BASIC WAYS to work rounds. In joined rounds, the last stitch of the round is slipstitched to the first stitch, and the next round begins evenly stepped up from the first. In spiral rounds, you simply continue to crochet in a continuous pattern. We'll start with joined rounds.

WORKING JOINED ROUNDS

To practice making joined rounds, we'll use double crochet stitches, starting with a base count of 12 double crochet stitches in the ring.

Setup. Chain 6. Slipstitch to the first chain to form your ring (see page 70).

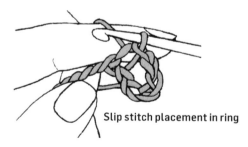

Slip stitch placement in ring

Round 1. Chain 2 (A). Place a stitch marker in the chain under your hook before beginning any of the other stitches, to help you identify the beginning of the round. Work 11 double crochets into the center of the ring. Note that because the chain-2 is not at an edge, you count it as a stitch. (This is almost always true when you're working joined rounds.) You now have 12 stitches in the round and your piece looks a bit like a pie that's missing a piece (B). Slipstitch into the uppermost chain of the chain-2 you began the round with; your stitch marker is here to

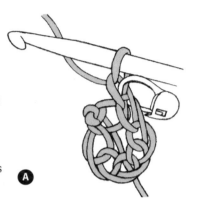

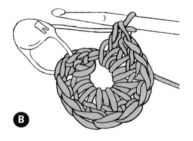

guide you. (*Note:* When slipstitching to join a round, it's important that you work under two strands of the chain and not just one, or the stitches will pull apart, and you will end up with a large hole where your join is.)

How to Begin Round 2

To understand where to place the first double crochet in Round 2, slowly pull out the chain-2 and the slip stitch you made at the beginning of the round. Note *where* you placed that slip stitch. You might want to keep track of that spot with a different-colored stitch marker. Make your slip stitch again and repeat your chain-2, and then make a double crochet stitch in the same chain where you placed the slip stitch to close Round 1. This stitch is needed because you must place 2 stitches in every stitch around and the chain-2 counts as a stitch. (It counts as a stitch in subsequent rounds as well.) This is the trickiest round; the rest are much easier.

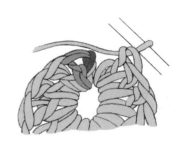

Round 2. Work a starting chain-2 (A), then work a double crochet in the same chain (see How to Begin Round 2, above).

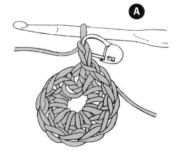

Work 2 double crochet stitches in the next stitch and in each stitch in Round 1 (B). Note that you are doubling the number of stitches you made in the ring in Round 1, to ensure that your crocheted circle lies flat. When you complete the round, you will have 24 double crochet stitches, counting the chain-1 as a stitch. Again, before joining the round, your piece will look a bit like a pie that's missing a slice (C). Slipstitch to the top (second) chain of your chain-2 to join the round (D).

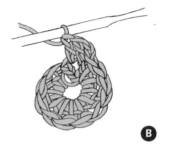

B

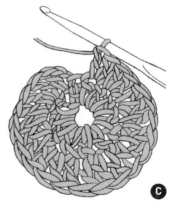

C

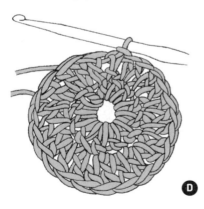

D

Ruffles and Cups

If your round begins to ruffle, you may have too many stitches, meaning you've increased too many times.

If your round begins to cup, you may have too few stitches, meaning you've missed an increase or two somewhere along the way.

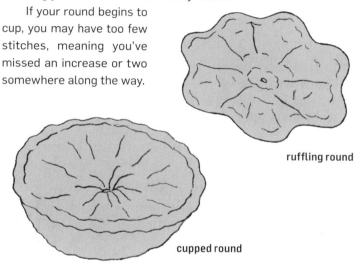

ruffling round

cupped round

Round 3. (*Note:* In Round 3, you do not double the number of stitches by placing 2 stitches in every stitch. Instead, you add 12 stitches, evenly spaced, by increasing in every other stitch. Remember: The starting chain counts as the first stitch.) Work a starting chain-2. Work 2 double crochet stitches in the next stitch (A). Work 1 double crochet in the next stitch, and 2 double crochets in the following stitch (B). Continue around in this manner, working a double crochet in the one stitch

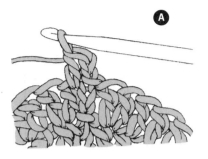

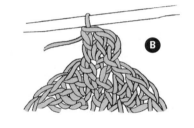

and then 2 double crochets in the following stitch, until you have a total of 36 stitches. Join with a slip stitch into the top (second) chain of the chain-2.

Continue in this manner for all subsequent rounds: for example, for Round 4, increase in every 3rd stitch; in Round 5, increase in every 4th stitch, and so on.

Working Joined Rounds in Single Crochet

Unlike when you're working in taller stitches, as just described for double crochet, if you're working in single crochet, you do not count the chain that begins the round as a stitch. When you come back around and need to slipstitch to join, place the slip stitch into the top of the first single crochet that you made. There just isn't enough substance to a single chain stitch for it to stand up on its own when worked in the round, but you still need it to position your hook correctly for single crochet stitches.

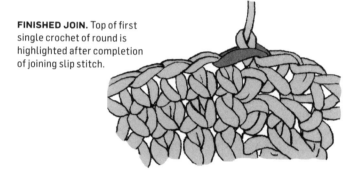

FINISHED JOIN. Top of first single crochet of round is highlighted after completion of joining slip stitch.

SPIRAL ROUNDS

THE INCREASE METHOD that you just learned for working joined rounds also applies to rounds worked in a spiral, with one exception: There are no chains or slip stitches to join.

WORKING SPIRAL ROUNDS

Setup. Start with 6 chains and slipstitch to the first chain to form your ring. Chain 2, but remember that this does not count as a stitch.

Round 1. Place 1 double crochet stitch into the ring. Stitch markers are essential when working in spirals to help you keep track of the first stitch of your round, so place a marker in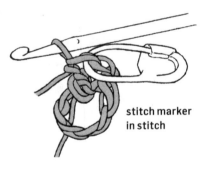

stitch marker in stitch

the top of this stitch exactly where you would slip your hook through to make a stitch. Work 11 more double crochet stitches into your ring.

Round 2. Since there are no slip stitches to join the rounds, work the first stitch of Round 2 into the marked stitch. You can take the stitch marker out before you place your new stitch, but then you'll want to put it back into the new stitch you have created, as this is your new beginning of the next round (A). Just as when you're working joined rounds, you need to work 2 stitches into each stitch around, so place a second stitch into the same spot, then work 2 double crochet stitches into each stitch around until you have 24 double crochet stitches. The next open stitch should be the marked stitch (B).

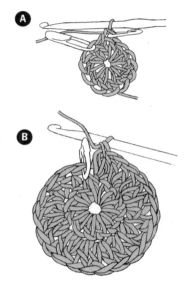

Round 3. Begin with a double crochet in the marked stitch. Remember to remove the marker and replace it in the top of the new stitch you have made, and work 2 double crochet stitches in the next stitch. Continue in the same manner as for working joined rounds: Work 1 double crochet in the next stitch and 2 in the following stitch, repeating this until you have 36 stitches.

CHAPTER 7

PERFECTING TECHNIQUES

In this chapter we'll cover some of the techniques that make you a better crocheter and your work more polished and professional looking. They include how to change yarns, hide ends, and add edgings, as well as methods for finishing your work.

CHANGING YARNS

ONCE YOU'VE DONE A BIT of crocheting, you're going to need to change yarns, whether to begin another color or simply to begin a new ball of yarn when you run out. Learning and practicing your options for how to do this are an important part of learning to crochet. Here are a few of the most common approaches.

- **At any point in the stitch.** While this is not elegant when changing colors because it splits the color of the stitch unevenly (see illustration on the facing page), it's completely acceptable if you're continuing with the same color but switching to a new skein or ball. This method is fine if you're working with a very dense stitch pattern or a highly textured yarn like mohair or fun fur. You don't want to use this method, however, if your stitch pattern is very open and lacey, or you are working with a smooth and shiny yarn, because the stitch in which the change happens will look slightly different than the surrounding stitches.

CHANGING YARN at any point in the stitch

- **At the end of a round or row.** Join a new color after you have finished a row or round and are beginning in a new spot. Insert your hook into your chosen, or indicated, stitch and pull through a loop of your new yarn (be sure to leave at least a 6-inch tail), and proceed with however many chains are required for the stitches you are using. This method works best when beginning a new round or row with an entirely new color or when you are joining onto a piece that has been completed.

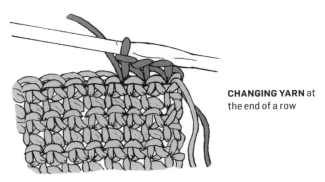

CHANGING YARN at the end of a row

- **Finish a stitch with the new yarn using a yarn over.** This is my favorite and the most effective option in almost every situation. This method is the same for all stitches: You change colors with the last yarn over of the stitch, no matter which stitch it is! I use this when changing balls but continuing with the same color. I also use it every time I need to change colors but don't necessarily need to fasten off the previous color. Let's try it first with single crochet.

USING A YARN OVER TO CHANGE YARNS IN SINGLE CROCHET

Step 1. Begin your next stitch by inserting your hook into the stitch; yarn over and bring up a loop.

CHANGING YARN with yarn over in single crochet

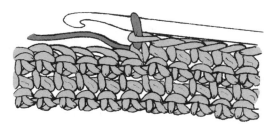

Step 2. Take the new color and fold the tail over (giving yourself at least a 6" tail) to make a loop. Grab this loop with your hook, and pull it through the 2 loops on your hook to complete the stitch you started. Cut the previous working yarn and continue working with your new color. This gives you a completed stitch in your old color, and the loop on your hook is in your new color. The next stitch will be completely in the new color.

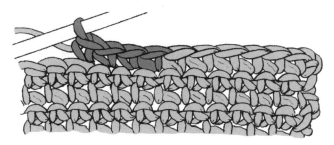

USING A YARNOVER TO CHANGE YARNS IN DOUBLE CROCHET

Step 1. Begin a stitch using your original yarn. Yarn over, insert your hook into the stitch, yarn over, and bring up a loop. Yarn over again and pull through 2 loops on your hook. Stop! The next step is the last yarn over of the double crochet stitch, and this is where you change color.

Step 2. Take the new yarn and fold the tail over, forming a loop. Grab this loop with your hook and pull through the 2 loops on your hook to complete the stitch.

You can weave in the ends when you've finished your project (see Anchoring Ends, page 96).

ADDING NEW yarn in double crochet

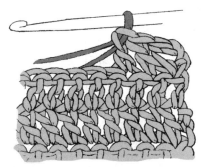

HIDING YOUR TAILS BY WORKING OVER THEM

CHANGING COLORS, or joining a new skein of the same color, leaves you with two unsightly tails, sometimes in the middle of your work. One of the lovely things about crochet is that you can work over these tails when you are using a solid stitch pattern and not have to worry about weaving or sewing them in at the end of the project.

Pick up a practice swatch and use it to experiment with changing colors. Work the point where you have a completed stitch and the loop on your hook is in the new color. Notice that the tails from both colors are hanging off the back of your work. Continue as follows:

Step 1. Bring both tails up so they sit just along the top of the stitches in the row below.

Step 2. Very carefully make your next single crochet stitch, keeping those tails just along that top edge. You aren't going to manipulate or move the two strands; they should just lie along the top of the last row the whole time you are making your new stitch so that they get trapped inside the single crochet stitch you are making; it forms a sort of tunnel around them.

HIDE TAILS along the top of the stitches.

Step 3. Continue to work about 2" worth of stitches over these tails. They should now be quite secure, so you can cut the ends and be done with them.

ADDING AN EDGE

ADDING A SIMPLE EDGE to even the humblest of crocheted squares can add a world of interest; it can also help even out the bit of scalloping that appears on the ends of rows, as well as disguise little inconsistencies in your tension.

You can use one of your practice swatches for this, but I suggest limiting the piece to 10 rows. If you have more than that, you can pull out the extra rows or simply start a new swatch and work until you have 10 rows of stitches, not counting your foundation chain. Make sure you have fastened off your original yarn (see When You Get to the End: Fastening Off, page 60). When you first practice adding an edge, use a yarn in a different color, so it will be easier to see what you're doing.

EDGING IN SINGLE CROCHET

You're going to work into this swatch starting in the upper right-hand corner with the right side of the last row you worked facing you. This sample edging is done in single crochet. For the purposes of learning how to add the edging and read your work, I recommend using a contrasting color. When finishing actual projects in the future, complete the first round or row of edging with the same color yarn.

Step 1. Join your edging yarn to the first stitch of the row (see page 84) (A). Chain 1 and place 1 single crochet stitch in that first stitch; continue to work 1 single crochet into each stitch along the top edge until the last stitch in the row (B).

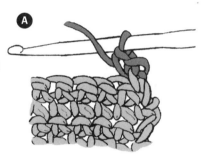

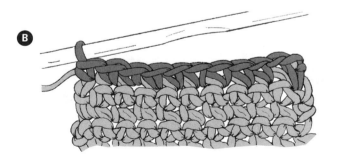

Step 2. Place 3 single crochet stitches in this last
stitch to turn the cor-
ner. Why 3 stitches in
the same place? Because
when you're working
around the edge of your
square you have quite a
distance to travel to get
around that corner and
still have it lie flat. You
need one stitch for one
side of your square, one
stitch for the other side of your square, and at least
one stitch to bridge the gap.

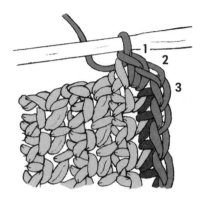

Step 3. On the next side, you work into the ends of rows and
not into the neat and tidy tops of stitches that you've gotten used to. The simplest way to anchor your stitches is

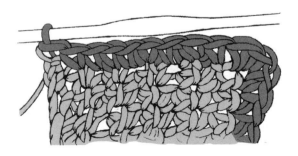

to work into the space between the last stitch of the row (at the edge) and the stitch previous to that in the same row. You should have one stitch per row, and since you have only 10 rows, you'll have a total of 10 stitches. *Note:* The third single crochet at the last corner counts as the first stitch for this side of your swatch.

Step 4. You're now ready to work along the bottom of your swatch into what's left of your foundation chain. Take a moment to look at your swatch right side up: Look at where each single crochet from that first row is anchored in your chain. Now flip it upside down: Can you still see where the stitches were worked into the chains? You're going to use those very same spots for the edge stitches on this side. If you find this difficult, you can place a stitch marker in each chain to help locate the right spot for working into the bottom of the chain.

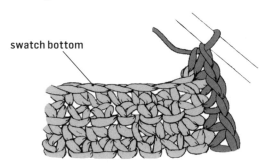

swatch bottom

Step 5. Place 3 single crochet stitches in the first chain stitch.

Step 6. Work one single crochet stitch in the bottom of each chain across.

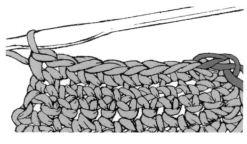

Step 7. On the fourth side, work in the ends of rows just as you did on the opposite side (step 3). Remember to place 3 single crochet stitches in the end of the first row you come to, and one single crochet stitch into the end of each row.

Step 8. When you reach the end of the fourth side, you are almost finished. Remember that you have placed 3 single crochet stitches in the first stitch of each side of the piece you're edging, but you did not start with 3 on the very first side. This is easy to remedy! Simply place 3 single crochet stitches in the last stitch of the last side. (For future projects you can begin your edging by placing 3 single crochet stitches in the very first stitch.)

Step 9. Slipstitch to the first single crochet you made to join the round. Fasten off (see page 60).

This process can be repeated with any of the stitches you've learned so far. The placement of the stitches is exactly the same as when you are working in single crochet, but the one change you do have to make is in the number of stitches that you work in the corners.

Hiding Attachments with Color

When adding an edge on a finished project, work the first round of your edging in the same color as your project. Any inconsistencies in the attachment of the edge will be hidden by the matching color. You can then add a second round of edging in a contrasting color if desired.

Edging with Other Stitches

Remember that when you worked in the round, the larger the stitches, the more stitches you needed to start with and to add in each round to keep the piece flat. The same principle applies when you are turning corners with edgings. Taller stitches make deeper corners and therefore need more stitches to cover them and still lie flat. As with single crochet, half double crochet requires 3 stitches per corner (A); double and treble crochet require 5 stitches per corner (B).

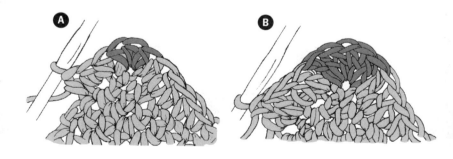

Handling Edgings along Side Rows

If you add an edging to a piece that was constructed with a stitch other than single crochet, you must work the row sides a little bit differently.

Half double crochet stitches are 1½ times as tall as single crochet stitches, so it follows you need 1½ stitches per row. Since it's impossible make a half stitch, you work 3 stitches for every 2 rows by alternately placing 1 stitch in the end of one row and then 2 stitches in the end of the next row.

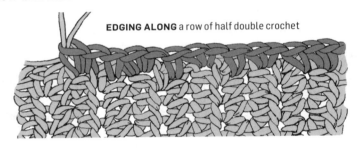

EDGING ALONG a row of half double crochet

Double crochet stitches are equal to 2 single crochet stitches in height, so instead of working one stitch into the end of each row, you must work 2.

EDGING ALONG a row of double crochet

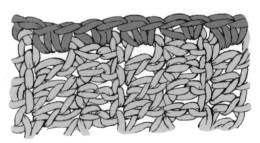

Treble crochet stitches are equal to 3 single crochet stitches in height, so instead of working one stitch into the end of each row, you must work 3.

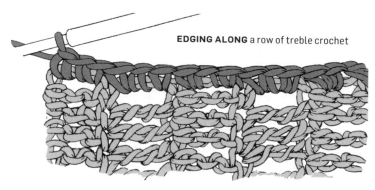

EDGING ALONG a row of treble crochet

After the first round, additional edging rounds are almost child's play because now you have stitches placed all the way around your piece, and the tops of the stitches are facing outward so you'll always be working into the tops of stitches. One stitch in each stitch, no more ends of rows! Just remember that you'll need to work the appropriate number of extra stitches in each corner so your piece lies flat.

FINISHING

FINISHING IS ABOUT POLISH — giving your work all the final little touches that make it complete. In this section, we learn how to anchor all those dangling ends by weaving them in, as well as how to block the finished item.

Anchoring Ends

Your first step in finishing your project is to weave in any ends, or tails, that you did not work into your piece already. There is quite a lot of yarn wrapped up and around itself in each crochet stitch, so weaving in your ends is as simple as burying those tails inside all that yarn. With single crochet, the stitches are already so dense that you can simply run your ends inside a row of stitches as if you had worked over the ends (see page 87).

ENDS RUN THROUGH single crochet with yarn needle

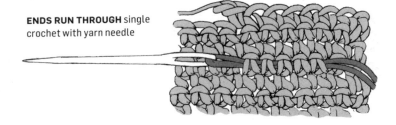

For all other stitches, work the yarn vertically through the body of one stitch across to the next and through that stitch vertically as well. With the more open nature of half double,

double, and treble crochet, it's important to change direction at least twice when weaving in your ends and to weave in no less than 2 inches of yarn to ensure that the ends are well secured.

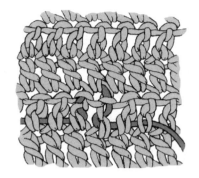

ENDS CHANGING DIRECTION to be securely woven in

Blocking

Your second finishing step is blocking. Yarn is an interesting object; before you begin crocheting with it, your yarn lives in nice, long, loopy loops in a ball or skein and thinks that its shape is long, loopy loops. After you've crocheted with it, it's all twisted up into little interlocking loops, but it still thinks it's supposed to be long, loopy loops. Blocking settles your stitches into their new shape.

There are two main methods for blocking: wet blocking and steam blocking. Which method you use should depend on not only the fiber, but also the project (see Fiber Matters, on the next page). For both methods, you need T-pins or pushpins and a blocking surface that you can sink pins into without damage and that can be damp while your piece dries. You can use a blocking board, a spare bed, or, for smaller items, an ironing board.

- **Wet blocking.** Soak your piece in lukewarm water with a no-rinse laundry wash, such as Soak or Eucalan, for 15 minutes. The wash helps to break the surface tension of the water so it can reach all the way into the core of the fibers that make up your yarn. It also leaves behind a little moisture to keep the fibers supple. Remove the piece from the water and gently squeeze the excess water from it. You may want to lay it on a towel, roll the towel up, and step on it to squeeze out as much extra water as possible. Lay your piece on the

Fiber Matters

Different fibers require different blocking methods.

- **Plant fibers.** Fibers such as cotton, bamboo, Tencel, and linen, all of which come from plants, have little to no "memory" or bounce, and so your stitches will tend to grow over time, especially in a larger project. The very weight of the yarn causes this distortion. It's therefore best to steam block these pieces, as getting them wet could cause so much distortion that your project would be ruined. If steam blocking is not available, be very careful when moving your piece from water to blocking surface. Hold it all together in a ball, and don't let any part sag.

- **Protein (animal) fibers.** Fibers such as wool, alpaca, mohair, angora, and llama can be either steam or wet blocked, although steam is the best method for alpaca. This is because alpaca has much less memory than some of the other animal fibers and thus may exhibit the same kind of "growth" that you'd find in a plant blocking surface and pin the edges to keep it in shape while it dries. Depending on how much water you removed and the ambient humidity, this can take anywhere from 12 hours to a couple of days.

- **Steam blocking.** With this method, you pin the edges of your piece first, and then with a clothing steamer (not a steam iron), gently steam the whole piece; let it cool and dry. This can take anywhere from 2 to 15 minutes.

....

fiber. With these fibers, the decision of which method to use is mostly dependent on the project. If it's a lace piece that you need to put under tension to open up the stitches, it's best to wet block it. This is because animal fibers stretch more easily when wet, so that if you try stretching a dry lacy piece to the correct measurements, you run the risk of breaking the yarn. For most other projects, laying the piece(s) down and gently pushing or pinning it into place before settling it with steam is perfectly fine.

- **Synthetic fibers,** such as acrylic, polymide, and nylon are typically not affected by blocking, and so it is not necessary to block them.

Note: If you are blocking a swatch, be sure to use the blocking method similar to the way you plan to treat the finished item. For instance, if you plan on washing a sweater, but steam block your gauge swatch for it, you may end up with different and possibly drastically disappointing results.

....

Once your piece is dry, unpin it and trim any remaining ends that you wove in prior to blocking. Now use or wear whatever fabulous piece of crochet you've just completed!

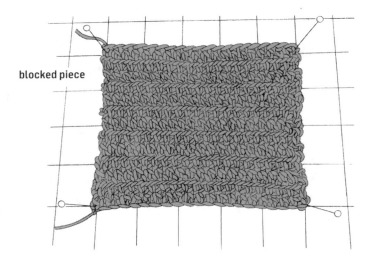

blocked piece

The Problem with Irons

Steam irons may seem like an acceptable way to steam block your work, but don't be fooled! An iron has a rocket-hot metal surface meant to be pressed to fabrics, and that hot metal can scorch your yarn and flatten its surface — neither of which you want. In addition, the purpose of blocking is to reset the memory of your yarn, to teach it a new shape. Your yarn has been stored in one of the four ways discussed on pages 11–12, and it thinks its shape is long loose loops. However, you've compressed and tangled it into many small interlocking loops, while the tension coiled in it is trying to pull it back to its previous shape. Wet blocking gets moisture all the way to the core of the fiber to help it relax into its new shape. When you use a steam iron, you have to do one of two things: Hold it far enough above your work so as not to scorch or melt the fibers with the hot iron's surface, or place a damp cloth or towel on your work to protect it, for the same reason. In either case, you are inhibiting the steam from really penetrating the fiber, so that the moisture is just hitting the surface of the yarn, and you're not actually blocking your piece. If a clothes steamer isn't available to you, use the wet blocking method.

CHAPTER 8

PATTERN READING

The final piece in learning how to crochet is reading patterns. Unless you are one of the few crocheters who thrive on and embrace free-form crochet style, you are going to want to make garments and accessories based on available patterns, which use abbreviations and other symbolic notations to provide information in a standardized and succinct written form.

This advice on reading patterns is followed by some basic patterns that you can use to make a few simple projects and try out your pattern-reading skills.

As you may have seen, crochet patterns seem not necessarily to be written in English, or in any other language for that matter. They are written in a series of numbers and abbreviations that allow a pattern to be transcribed with maximum information and minimum text. Always make sure you check the abbreviations and notations in your pattern, and know what they mean before you begin the project. I'm going to try to help you decipher these codes using the following examples, first with patterns in rows, followed by patterns worked in rounds.

Because crochet patterns are like a language of their own, as with any language, you'll find dialects in different regions with subtle varying differences. When designers write out their patterns, their "dialects" show. The patterns included here indicate a repeat by saying "repeat from * six times more." This can also be written as "repeat from * for a total of eight repeats," or as "repeat from * across/around." Before you begin a new project, take time to read through your pattern to familiarize

---

Important Notations

Asterisk (*). This marks the beginning of a section of the pattern instructions that you will repeat.

Parentheses ( ). There is information between the parentheses about whatever stitch or pattern instructions immediately preceded them.

Brackets [ ]. These are used when there's a series of stitches that need to happen all together. Although you won't encounter them in this book, you will see them in crochet patterns beyond the beginner level. They function the same way that grouped math functions do: for instance, (4 + 2) × 2. You don't multiply by 2 until you have finished the equation in the parentheses. Bracketed crochet instructions are handled the same way; for instance, [3 dc, ch 3, 3 dc] in the next ch-3 sp, means that *everything* within those brackets happens together in the next ch-3 space.

---

yourself with the language that the designer uses, so you aren't confused midpattern when you encounter a phrase or instruction you've never seen before.

Most Common Crochet Abbreviations

Most patterns include the abbreviations that you need to know to complete the project. You can also find a comprehensive list of crochet abbreviations through the Crochet Guild of America (www. crochet.org) or the Craft Yarn Council (www.craftyarncouncilcom).

ch	chain	dc	double crochet
hdc	half double crochet	rs	right side
sl st	slipstitch	sc	single crochet
sp	space	st(s)	stitch(es)
tr	treble crochet	ws	wrong side
yo	yarn over		

PATTERNS FOR ROWS

FOR PRACTICE FOLLOWING INSTRUCTIONS in a pattern that is worked in rows, review the instructions on page 106 for making a single crochet swatch. Now, compare those instructions with the table on the facing page, which shows (in the first column) what you would generally expect to find in formal crochet instructions and (in the second column) a breakdown of what's meant — a "translation"!

When you are beginning to work with patterns, it can be helpful to write these instructions out in longhand for yourself, but keep the original pattern handy. The more often you reference the pattern as written, in its highly abbreviated state, the sooner the language of crochet patterns will begin to make sense to you. Remember, just as when you took the very first steps in learning to crochet, it takes time, patience, and practice to build this new skill.

Single Crochet Practice Swatch

	TYPICAL PATTERN		TRANSLATION
SETUP	Ch 11	SETUP	Chain 11; this is your foundation chain of 10 plus the turning chain for single crochet.
ROW 1	Sc in 2nd ch from hook and in each st across. (10 sc)	ROW 1	Work 1 single crochet in the 2nd chain from the hook and 1 single crochet in each chain across. (10 single crochet stitches total)
ROW 2	Ch 1, turn, sc in each st across. (10 sc)	ROW 2	Chain 1 and turn the piece over; work 1 single crochet in each stitch across. (10 single crochet stitches total)
ROWS 3–10	Repeat Row 2 eight times more; fasten off (see page 60).	ROWS 3–10	Repeat Row 2 eight times more. Fasten off (see page 60) the last stitch.

ROW-BY-ROW FORMULAS FOR 4-INCH SQUARES

These little sample projects make great coasters and washcloths. Make bunches of them to sew together into placemats, pillow covers, or blankets. Use the same worsted-weight or DK cotton and hook that you have been using to practice the stitches and techniques in the previous chapters, and use any of the stitches you've learned in chapter 4.

FOR SINGLE CROCHET

Setup Ch 31 (or the correct number to give you a chain that is 4" wide, plus 1). Note the number of chains you have made before the plus-1; this is how many single crochet stitches you will work in each row.

Row 1 Sc in 2nd ch from hook and in each st across. (30 sc)

Row 2 Ch 1, turn, sc in each st across. (30 sc)

Repeat Row 2 twenty-eight times more; fasten off (see page 60). (30 rows total)

Note: To make a square in single crochet, the number of rows worked is equal to the number of single crochet stitches in each row. If you work more or fewer than 30 stitches in each row, you should work an equal number of rows.

single crochet swatch

FOR HALF DOUBLE CROCHET

Setup Ch 32 (or the correct number to give you a chain that is 4" wide, plus 2). Note the number of chains you have made before the plus-2; this is how many half double crochet stitches you will work in each row.

Row 1 Hdc in 3rd ch from hook and in each st across. (30 hdc)

Row 2 Ch 2, turn, hdc in each st across. (30 hdc)

Repeat Row 2 eighteen times more; fasten off (see page 60). (20 rows total)

Note: To make a square in half double crochet, divide the number of stitches worked by 1.5; that is the number of rows

half double
crochet
swatch

you need; you may need to round up or down. (Half double crochet stitches are 1.5 times as tall as they are wide.) In this pattern, if each row includes more or fewer than 30 stitches, you may need to change the total number of rows worked.

FOR DOUBLE CROCHET

Setup Ch 32 (or the correct number to give you a chain that is 4" wide, plus 2). Note the number of chains you have made before the plus-2; this is how many double crochet stitches you will work in each row.

Row 1 Dc in 3rd ch from hook and in each st across. (30 dc)

double
crochet
swatch

Row 2 Ch 2, turn, dc in each st across. (30 dc)

Repeat Row 2 thirteen times more; fasten off (see page 60). (15 rows total)

Note: Since double crochet stitches are twice as tall as they are wide, work half as many rows as the number of stitches to make a square in double crochet.

FOR TREBLE CROCHET

Setup Ch 33 (or the correct number to give you a chain that is 4" wide, plus 3). Note the number of chains you have made before the plus-3; this is how many treble crochet stitches you will work in each row.

Row 1 Tr in 4th ch from hook and in each st across. (30 tr)

Row 2 Ch 3, turn, tr in each st across. (30 tr)

Repeat Row 2 eight times more; fasten off (see page 60). (10 rows total)

Note: To make a square in treble crochet, divide the number of stitches worked by 3 to determine the number of rows you need (rounding up or down as needed).

treble crochet swatch

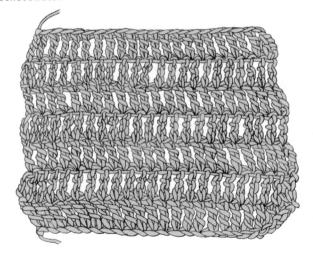

PATTERNS FOR ROUNDS

To practice following typical crochet instructions for working in rounds, go back to pages 69–71 and review the instructions for making a circle in double crochet. Now compare these to the typical crochet instructions shown in the left-hand column of the table below. As with the row-by-row instructions, this can look like crazy technical jargon at first — and in a way it is! But break it down line by line until you can read it easily, referring to the "translation" in the right-hand column. Remember to write out the pattern in longhand and also to reference the pattern as originally written, until the language of crochet becomes familiar and readable to you.

Double Crochet Practice Rounds

	TYPICAL PATTERN		TRANSLATION
SETUP	Ch 6, sl st to form a ring.	SETUP	Chain 6 and slipstitch to your first chain stitch to form a ring.
ROUND 1	Ch 2 (counts as dc on all rounds), 11 dc into ring, join with sl st to 2nd ch of ch-2. (12 dc)	ROUND 1	Chain 2 (this chain-2 counts as a double crochet stitch in this round and in all that follow), make 11 double crochet stitches anchored into the center of the ring; join the circle by placing a slip stitch in the top (or 2nd) chain of the chain-2 that you started with. (12 double crochet stitches around)

	TYPICAL PATTERN		TRANSLATION
ROUND 2	Ch 2, dc in same ch (or st), 2 dc in each st around, join with sl st to 2nd ch of ch-2. (24 dc)	ROUND 2	Chain 2, place one double crochet in the same stitch that this chain-2 originates from (where you placed the slip stitch that closed the previous round), place 2 double crochet stitches in each remaining stitch around, join the circle by placing a slip stitch in the top (2nd) chain of the chain-2 that you started with. (24 double crochet stitches around)
ROUND 3	Ch 2, 2 dc in next st, *1 dc in next st, 2 dc in following st; repeat from * 10 times more, join with sl st to 2nd ch of ch-2. (36 dc)	ROUND 3	Chain 2, place 2 double crochet stitches in the next stitch, * place one double crochet in the next stitch, place 2 double crochet stitches in the following stitch; repeat from the asterisk 10 times more, join the circle by placing a slip stitch in the top (2nd) chain of the chain-2 that you started with. (36 double crochet stitches around)
ROUND 4	Ch 2, dc in next st, 2 dc in following st, *1 dc in each of next 2 sts, 2 dc in following st; repeat from * 10 times more, join with sl st to 2nd ch of ch-2. (48 dc)	ROUND 4	Chain 2, place one double crochet in the next stitch and 2 double crochet stitches in the following stitch, * place one double crochet in each of the next 2 stitches, place 2 double crochet stitches in the following stitch; repeat from the asterisk 10 times more, join the circle by placing a slip stitch in the top (2nd) chain of the chain-2 that you started with. (48 double crochet stitches around)

TYPICAL PATTERN	TRANSLATION
ROUND 5 Ch 2, dc in each of next 2 sts, 2 dc in following st, *1 dc in each of next 3 sts, 2 dc in following st; repeat from * 10 times more, join with sl st to 2nd ch of ch-2. (60 dc) Fasten off.	**ROUND 5** Chain 2, place one double crochet in each of the next 2 stitches and 2 double crochet stitches in the following stitch, * place one double crochet in each of the next 3 stitches, place 2 double crochet stitches in the following stitch; repeat from the asterisk 10 times more, join the circle by placing a slip stitch in the top (2nd) chain of the chain-2 that you started with. (60 double crochet stitches around). Cut your yarn and secure the last loop.

ROUND-BY-ROUND FORMULAS
FOR 4-INCH CIRCLES

Now practice your pattern-reading skills by following the instructions below to make some more sample projects. Like the 4-inch squares on the previous page, these little rounds can make great coasters and washcloths. Use the same worsted-weight cotton and hook that you have been using to practice the stitches and techniques in previous chapters, and complete them using any stitch you want.

FOR SINGLE CROCHET

Setup Ch 6, sl st to form a ring.

Round 1 Ch 1, 8 sc into ring, join with sl st to first sc. (8 sc)

Round 2 Ch 1, sc in same st, 2 sc in each st around, join with sl st to first sc. (16 sc)

Round 3 Ch 1, 2 sc in next st, *sc in next st, 2 sc in following st; repeat from * six times more, join with sl st to first sc. (24 sc)

Round 4 Ch 1, sc in next st, 2 sc in following st, *sc in each of next 2 sts, 2 sc in following st; repeat from * six times more, join with sl st to first sc. (32 sc)

Round 5 Ch 1, sc in each of next 2 sts, 2 sc in following st, *sc in each of next 3 sts, 2 sc in following st; repeat from * six times more, join with sl st to first sc. (40 sc)

Round 6 Ch 1, sc in each of next 3 sts, 2 sc in following st, *sc in each of next 4 sts, 2 sc in following st; repeat from * six times more, join with sl st to first sc. (48 sc)

Round 7 Ch 1, sc in each of next 4 sts, 2 sc in following st, *sc in each of next 5 sts, 2 sc in following st; repeat from * six times more, join with sl st to first sc. (56 sc)

Round 8 Ch 1, sc in each of next 5 sts, 2 sc in following st, *sc in each of next 6 sts, 2 sc in following st; repeat from * six times more, join with sl st to first sc. (64 sc)

Round 9 Ch 1, sc in each of next 6 sts, 2 sc in following st, *sc in each of next 7 sts, 2 sc in following st; repeat from * six times more, join with sl st to first sc. (72 sc)

Round 10 Ch 1, sc in each of next 7 sts, 2 sc in following st, *sc in each of next 8 sts, 2 sc in following st; repeat from * six times more, join with sl st to first sc. (80 sc)

Round 11 Ch 1, sc in each of next 8 sts, 2 sc in following st, *sc in each of next 9 sts, 2 sc in following st; repeat from * six times more, join with sl st to first sc. (88 sc)

single crochet circle

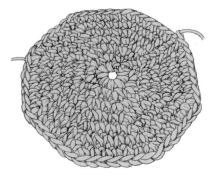

Round 12 Ch 1, sc in each of next 9 sts, 2 sc in following st, *sc in each of next 10 sts, 2 sc in following st; repeat from * six times more, join with sl st to first sc. (96 sc)

Round 13 Ch 1, sc in each of next 10 sts, 2 sc in following st, *sc in each of next 11 sts, 2 sc in following st; repeat from * six times more, join with sl st to first sc. (104 sc)

Round 14 Ch 1, sc in each of next 11 sts, 2 sc in following st, *sc in each of next 12 sts, 2 sc in following st; repeat from * six times more, join with sl st to first sc. (112 sc)

Round 15 Ch 1, sc in each of next 12 sts, 2 sc in following st, *sc in each of next 13 sts, 2 sc in following st; repeat from * six times more, join with sl st to first sc. (120 sc)

FOR HALF DOUBLE CROCHET

Setup Ch 6, sl st to form a ring.

Round 1 Ch 2 (counts as hdc on this and all rounds), 9 hdc into ring, join with sl st to 2nd ch of ch-2. (10 hdc)

Round 2 Ch 2, hdc in same st, 2 hdc in each st around, join with sl st to 2nd ch of ch-2. (20 hdc)

Round 3 Ch 2, 2 hdc in next st, *hdc in next st, 2 hdc in following st; repeat from * eight times more, join with sl st to 2nd ch of ch-2. (30 hdc)

Round 4 Ch 2, hdc in next st, 2 hdc in following st, *hdc in each of next 2 sts, 2 hdc in following st; repeat from * eight times more, join with sl st to 2nd ch of ch-2. (40 hdc)

Round 5 Ch 2, hdc in each of next 2 sts, 2 hdc in following st, *hdc in each of next 3 sts, 2 hdc in following st; repeat from * eight times more, join with sl st to 2nd ch of ch-2. (50 hdc)

Round 6 Ch 2, hdc in each of next 3 sts, 2 hdc in following st, *hdc in each of next 4 sts, 2 hdc in following st; repeat from * eight times more, join with sl st to 2nd ch of ch-2. (60 hdc)

Round 7 Ch 2, hdc in each of next 4 sts, 2 hdc in following st, *hdc in each of next 5 sts, 2 hdc in following st; rep from * eight times more, join with sl st to 2nd ch of ch-2. (70 hdc)

Round 8 Ch 2, hdc in each of next 5 sts, 2 hdc in following st, *hdc in each of next 6 sts, 2 hdc in following st; repeat from * eight times more, join with sl st to 2nd ch of ch-2. (80 hdc)

Round 9 Ch 2, hdc in each of next 6 sts, 2 hdc in following st, *hdc in each of next 7 sts, 2 hdc in following st; repeat from * eight times more, join with sl st to 2nd ch of ch-2. (90 hdc)

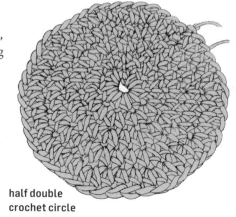

half double crochet circle

Round 10 Ch 2, hdc in each of next 7 sts, 2 hdc in following st, *hdc in each of next 8 sts, 2 hdc in following st; repeat from * eight times more, join with sl st to 2nd ch of ch-2. (100 hdc)

FOR DOUBLE CROCHET

Setup Ch 6, sl st to form a ring.

Round 1 Ch 2 (counts as dc on this and all rounds), 11 dc into ring, join with sl st to 2nd ch of ch-2. (12 dc)

Round 2 Ch 2, dc in same st, 2 dc in each st around, join with sl st to 2nd ch of ch-2. (24 dc)

Round 3 Ch 2, 2 dc in next st, *dc in next st, 2 dc in following st; repeat from * 10 times more, join with sl st to 2nd ch of ch-2. (36 dc)

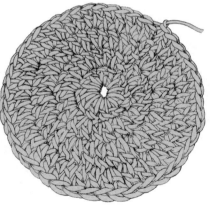

double crochet circle

Round 4 Ch 2, dc in next st, 2 dc in following st, *dc in each of next 2 sts, 2 dc in following st; repeat from * 10 times more, join with sl st to 2nd ch of ch-2. (48 dc)

Round 5 Ch 2, dc in each of next 2 sts, 2 dc in following st, *dc in each of next 3 sts, 2 dc in following st; repeat from * 10 times more, join with sl st to 2nd ch of ch-2. (60 dc)

Round 6 Ch 2, dc in each of next 3 sts, 2 dc in following st, *dc in each of next 4 sts, 2 dc in following st; repeat from * 10 times more, join with sl st to 2nd ch of ch-2. (72 dc)

Round 7 Ch 2, dc in each of next 4 sts, 2 dc in following st, *dc in each of next 5 sts, 2 dc in following st; repeat from * 10 times more, join with sl st to 2nd ch of ch-2. (84 dc)

FOR TREBLE CROCHET

Setup Ch 6, sl st to form a ring.

Round 1 Ch 3 (counts as tr on this and all rounds), 15 tr into ring, join with sl st to 3rd ch of ch-3. (16 tr)

Round 2 Ch 3, tr in same st, 2 tr in each st around, join with sl st to 3rd ch of ch-3. (32 tr)

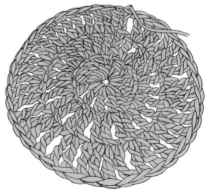

Round 3 Ch 3, 2 tr in next st, *tr in next st, 2 tr in following st; repeat from * fourteen times more, join with sl st to 3rd ch of ch-3. (48 tr)

treble crochet circle

Round 4 Ch 3, tr in next st, 2 tr in following st, *tr in each of next 2 sts, 2 tr in following st; repeat from * 14 times more, join with sl st to 3rd ch of ch-3. (64 tr)

Round 5 Ch 3, tr in each of next 2 sts, 2 tr in following st, *tr in each of next 3 sts, 2 tr in following st; repeat from * 14 times more, join with sl st to 3rd ch of ch-3.

....

Variations

• Add some interest by completing the last round in a contrasting color, or add stripes by changing color at the beginning of any round (see page 84).

• Make larger pieces by continuing to increase in the same pattern, by adding one additional stitch between increases in each round.

• Turn these rounds into the base of a bag or basket at any time; when the circle is as wide as you'd like the bag to be, simply stop increasing. If you work a consistent number of stitches in each round, you will see the sides of your bag grow upward in a cylinder shape. Just keep adding rounds until the piece is as deep as you'd like it to be.

• You can easily add handles or a strap to your basket or bag. Single crochet is the best stitch to use for this purpose, as it's the strongest and sturdiest of the stitches and can take the wear and tear of usage best. Simply crochet a strip or two in the width and length that you'd like, and sew to the top edge of your piece.

....

RESOURCES

USEFUL WEBSITES

Craft Yarn Council
www.craftyarncouncil.com
Here you will find all the industry standards for yarn gauge, how yarns are labeled, standard measurements for babies and adult sizes, as well as free patterns, basic techniques, and community support.

Crochet Guild of America
www.crochet.org
This is your home if you get hooked on crochet! These are your people! Keep up to date with what's happening in crochet, events around the country, and lots of support from other crocheters, as well as their Crochet Masters program. Additionally, if you become a member, you'll receive a subscription to their magazine, *Crochet!,* which is full of new patterns and lots of great resource articles.

Crochet Me Interweave Press
www.crochetme.com
The online home of *Interweave Crochet,* this site has lots of great patterns and how-tos, as well as a formidable backlist of issues chockful of amazing patterns and techniques. This is a great magazine to have a traditional or e-subscription to.

Ravelry
www.ravelry.com
An amazing online resource for knitters and crocheters, with thousands of patterns listed, some for sale directly through the site. Here you will find info on yarns new and old, designers whom you can contact directly, and lots of forums to find help, kvetch, or discuss your favorite things.

WEBS
www.yarn.com
WEBS not only sells yarn, books, patterns, and accessories through their website, but they also offers how-to videos and classes, if you're local to their retail store.

READING LIST

Budd, Ann. *The Crocheter's Handy Guide to Yarn Requirements.* Interweave. Always a great little pamphlet to keep in your purse or knitting bag, it has yardage estimates in different yarn weights for lots of different kinds of projects.

Schapper, Linda P. *Complete Book of Crochet Stitch Designs,* rev. ed. Lark Crafts, 2011. This is one of the best stitch dictionaries. There are 500 stitch patterns to choose from, all presented with wonderfully simple photographs, well-written pattern repeats, and charts.

The following books offer variations on the basics of yarn and tools, as well as basic stitches and advanced techniques. These little books are like having a crochet instructor in your pocket! Can't remember which seam to use? How to weave in ends? Although not necessarily how-to books, they are all great sources of information if you need a refresher or quick reminder on a technique. Take the time to look through them and find the format that appeals to you most. Once you have, tuck that copy in your project bag.

Brown, Nancy. *The Crocheter's Companion,* rev. ed. Interweave, 2013.

Chin, Lily. *Lily Chin's Crochet Tips & Tricks.* Potter Craft, 2009.

Eckman, Edie. *The Crochet Answer Book.* Storey Publishing, 2005.

ACKNOWLEDGMENTS

My thanks to:

WEBS, for being MY yarn store and the most incredible place I have ever worked.

Leslie Ann Bestor — that was one heck of a door you opened!

My girls for helping me make practice patches for so many classes and for letting me hide in the studio all those weekends to write.

And to Patrick, because reasons.

INDEX

Italics indicates an illustration; **bold** indicates a table or chart.